FRANCE

Its People and Culture

Lynn M. Hilton, Ph.D.
Editor-in-Chief

Contents

National Textbook Company
a division of *NTC Publishing Group* • Lincolnwood, Illinois USA

Preface

The authors of *Focus on Europe* have created eleven clear, comprehensive introductions to the people and cultures of Western European countries. Each book provides a look into the past and present history, art, literature, and politics of a nation—all in one compact source. These books are ideal for those making their first contacts with a country or group of countries.

This revised and updated edition of *France: its People and Culture* provides up-to-date information on the French government, culture, and even popular music. Business travelers and tourists alike will gain insights from this book into the culture of the country in which they plan to spend time or do business. Beginning students of French will benefit from the wide range of subjects treated as they make their first contact with French culture; advanced students will find comprehensive essays on important historical and cultural topics that will help them deepen their understanding of the French people.

France: Its People and Culture, like the other books in the *Focus on Europe* series, will offer much toward the understanding of the great traditions of a country and will help readers to a richer, more profound understanding of a European culture.

Published by National Textbook Company, a division of NTC Publishing Group.

Library of Congress Catalog Card Number: 76-159547
Manufactured in the United States of America.

4 5 6 7 8 9 0 ML 9 8 7 6 5 4 3 2 1

The storming of the Bastille, July 14, 1789, marks the beginning of the French Revolution.

The History of France

R. L. Walker

France provides fertile ground for the student of history. Perhaps more than any other European nation, France's past remains alive and integrated with the present. Because the French are individualists, they have stubbornly retained from the past what they believed to be worthwhile.

France is a nation of distinct regional differences, and each area has retained and incorporated its own version of France's history. For example, in the little village of Les Girouteaux, the folk live in walled-up caves that have been inhabited for the last 50,000 years and light these cozy homes with electricity. In a like manner, all of France is a fascinating patchwork quilt of past and present, and in order to have even the smallest understanding of the France of today one must have a knowledge of its yesterdays. Generously, France carries its yesterdays, as well as the history of all Western civilization, as openly as rustics display the harvests of their fields.

Within France's natural borders—the Atlantic, Rhine River, Alps, Mediterranean, and Pyrenees, succeeding ages have entered this natural amphitheater, played their roles, and clearly left their marks, beginning with the dawn of civilization a hundred thousand years ago. Les Eyzies en Dordogne on the Vezere River was the Stone Age capital of a paleolithic nation that lived along the western edge of the Massif Central. Standing among the limestone rocks in the valley of the Vezere, it is not difficult to imagine our ancestors huddled around protective fires, listening to the sounds of the fearsome, man-eating tiger and gigantic mastodon. The world was a strange mixture of beauty and danger, of poetry and violence.

These early men not only survived but laid the foundations of our civilization. Early horses, mammoths, and reindeer were the food supply of these primitive hunters, who used stone-tipped spears, stone axes, or guile to kill their prey. These hunters and their families lived in the limestone caves that dot the valley. However, the caves provided free entry to all creatures, and the hunters often became the prey of monstrous cave bears, giant hyenas, and huge cats.

The caves of the Vezere valley have preserved the finest known examples of paleolithic settlements. In these caves early man left his tools, his ornaments, and his bones, which indicate a burial ritual and belief in the soul—and, most exciting of all, his art. In the *grottes* of Font-de-Gaume and Lascaux, paintings of bison, horses, and reindeer seem to thunder across the walls and ceilings, attesting to the high creative ability of these early men. In about the third millennium B.C., agriculture was transmitted to this region via the peoples of the Mediterranean.

The Ligurians

France saw the birth of a new community of men called Ligurians by the Greeks who knew of them. The civilization of the Ligurians centered in the Rhone basin and lakes of the Alpine region. They built fortifications and storehouses in the center of a body of water and were known as lake dwellers. Beyond the lakes, their settlements were surrounded by pastures and fields. The Ligurians were an olive-skinned, dark-haired people of short stature who were strongly attached to the soil. They were famous throughout the ancient world as swift runners, and the word Ligurian became a synonym for fleetness. The earth, sun, moon, stars, and fire were worshipped as deities by the Ligurians, and huge monuments of polished stone were raised over the mass graves of the dead. Corn, barley, and flax were major crops, while pigs, sheep, and goats comprised their stock. Clothing of flax or wool replaced the furs of earlier man, and bread was made.

Although the people we call French today are basically of Ligurian origin, the Celts were the second largest group in the population mix.

Originally from the area around the Baltic, the Celts, who called themselves Galates, spent most of the fifth century B.C. conquering the Ligurians, who greatly outnumbered them. But the Ligurian defenses were not sufficient for the howling, mass attacks of the Celts. The Celts, or Gauls, imposed their rule on the natives but, in turn, adopted many Ligurian customs. In contrast to the Ligurians, the Gauls were tall, fair, and blue-eyed.

It was said of the Gauls that their two greatest loves were fighting and talking. To a certain extent the same is true today; give a Frenchman an argument and he's a happy man.

The basis of the social organization was the family, headed by the father, who held life-and-death power. Several families formed a clan, several clans a tribe, and several tribes a nation. Each tribe rendered obedience to common chiefs, held common traditions, lived in a common territory, and worshiped common gods. The chiefs of the various tribes or nations formed councils which decided broad courses of action and policy. Tribe differed from tribe, depending upon the regions that shaped them. The tribe near Bourges were miners; other tribes excelled in pottery. Some tribes, like the Parasii, were sailors—or, like the Rimi, were known for their fine horses.

Although each tribe retained economic independence (based on agriculture), occasionally one tribe would promise gifts and loyalty to another in return for protection in case of war. Here were the roots of feudalism. The Gauls had no cities as such, but they had centers where councils met, provisions were stored, and markets held. Homes were made of wood, reeds, and mud, and resembled beehives. Bread, then as now, was the basic staple of their diet. Clothes were brightly colored and very similar in style to the trousers and wide-sleeved smock still worn by French peasants.

Druidism was the religion of the Galates, and like the Ligurians they worshiped natural phenomena. The beech, oak, and mistletoe were thought to be endowed with supernatural powers, and many places held sacred by the Ligurians retained their holiness with the Gauls. The druids or priests were a learned group and were divided into three classes: those who officiated at rituals, bards or poets, and healers. The teachings of the druids were reserved for the noble class of rulers and were transmitted by oral poems. Since the Gauls had no writing, their history, lore, medicine, and philosophy were transmitted from one generation to the next orally and from memory. The druids acted as judges as well as priests, and the worst possible punishment was excommunication or ostracism from the rest of the group. Sacrifice was demanded as a part of ritual, including human sacrifice, and the Gauls heaped treasures of gold, silver, and gems into sacred groves or lakes. The Romans record collecting as much as $100,000 in gold and silver after dredging the sacred lakes, and this may have been one of the reasons Caesar was so warmly greeted when he returned to Rome following his conquest of Gaul.

The Roman Conquest

By the time Rome was strong enough to decide upon the conquest of Gaul, the tribes of Gaul were jealously squabbling among themselves on a regular basis. Not forgetting their past victories over Roman armies, they felt more threatened by the Teutonic hordes that pushed at the boundary of the Rhine. Some Germans finally broke across the border, and this, combined with the migration of a Celtic tribe from Switzerland, was all that the young, ambitious Julius Caesar needed to convince the Roman senate to place troops at his disposal to "protect" Rome's Gallic allies. In 58 B.C., Caesar and his army crossed the St. Bernard pass, the Gauls little realizing their independence was at stake.

Caesar himself best tells the story of the subjugation of Gaul in his *Conquest of Gaul*. He begins his narrative with "All of Gaul is divided into three parts," and it was this division that brought Gaul's defeat. But the conquest was not an easy one; the Romans had to deal with the country as well as the Gallic warriors. Most of Gaul was a vast forest with thick undergrowth, interrupted by marshes and bogs, and it was said that soldiers could march through the forest of Ardennes for sixty days and find no end. The wars in Gaul, which lasted ten years, resulted in a million Gauls dead, a million enslaved, and a million left to rebuild their devastated country. At the foot of a statue raised in Gaul to Vercingetorix, the heroic young chieftain who tried to unite the Gauls but died in battle with Caesar, Caesar's words were engraved: "United, Gaul would have defied the world."

At the end of the Gallic Wars, Rome busily set about imposing its civilization upon the Gauls. In the area near Nîmes and Arles are found the best examples of Roman architecture outside Rome itself. These remnants of Rome's presence still speak of the power the empire imposed on Gaul for 500 years. The upper classes gave up their religion, customs, and language and adopted those of Rome; however, the lower classes clung to many of their traditional ways. Roman law was substituted for druidic law and the tribal system was replaced by a magistrate and his tribunals. A Roman governor was appointed to each province and had the power to tax the people as he saw fit. In many cases this power was extremely overexercised.

Cities were established by the Romans, and Lyon was built as the economic and political capital of Gaul. *City* to the Romans meant a town plus its surrounding estates, villages, fields, pastures, and woods. The cities were busy places and contained a variety of structures. Each town had a forum, a basilica, public baths, a theater, arena, and temples to Roman gods and emperors.

Many French historians contend that, in the long run, the Gauls contributed more to the Roman civilization than the Romans did to theirs. The Celto-Ligurian belief in the immortal soul was transmitted to the Romans. Soap was invented by the Gauls, as well as superior vegetable dyes, the mechanical reaper, and the art of enameling. In fact, the Gauls were such superior producers of a great variety of goods that Marseilles was the busiest seaport of the Roman world outside of Italy.

Marseilles was founded as a trading colony in the seventh century B.C. by the Phoenicians. It later became the Greek headquarters for trade with the western Mediterranean, and so expanded in size that Greek colonists founded suburbs nearby, such as Nice and Antibes. Rome used Marseilles as a military base as well as a port. From Marseilles the Romans shipped tin (transported through Gaul from Britain), copper, iron, gray amber, coral, the fine Gallic glassware, and the Gallic inventions already mentioned. The Romans adopted and imported Gallic clothing and carts and carriages designed and manufactured by the Gauls. Gallic salt pork was a Roman favorite and Gallic barley beer rivaled wine in popularity. In this way much of Gaul was put to work tilling the soil or tending herds to feed Roman stomachs and working at looms or in shops to manufacture goods to satisfy the Roman love of luxury. Christianity provided the first effective counterforce to Roman rule, and it is probable that the first Christian church in Gaul was founded in Marseilles.

Christianity

Christianity took hold of the Gauls slowly but, once gained, the hold was strong. Although Christianity easily replaced the worship of Roman deities, it was much more difficult for it to replace the firmly rooted belief in the mystical powers of trees, springs, and mistletoe. However, Christian doctrine began to be preached in the vernacular, and the ranks of the faithful swelled. Martyrs were inspirational models of the powers of faith, and Roman persecution converted many to the faith.

An example of the power of martyrdom is provided by St. Blandine, a slave girl of Lyon. In the agony of Roman-inflicted torture, she constantly repeated in a calm voice "I am a Christian, and nothing wrong is done amongst us."She was then thrown into the arena to wild beasts, which attacked her but refused to kill her. Blandine was then burned with hot irons, put into a net, and thrown to a wild bull. The bull tossed her into the air, then left her alone. When she fell back to the ground the same calm voice was still repeating "I am a Christian, and nothing wrong is done amongst us." She was finally beheaded.

The persecution of Christians continued until the collapse of the Roman Empire, not because of the religious doctrines of Christianity as such but because its beliefs were subversive to the economic and political foundations of Rome. By the time Teutonic tribes finally broke across the Rhine in large numbers, Christianity had a firm foothold in Gaul.

Gaul was the major corridor of the barbarians' invasions of the Roman Empire, and because of the presence of Roman legions over several centuries, the Gauls had lost the practice of warfare and were unable to defend themselves or their Roman masters. The barbarians built no towns and lived a primitive life of hunting and pasturage, which required vast territories of land to support the population.

Under the pressure of expanding population and migratory hordes from the east, the Germans looked to the land in Gaul. In about A.D. 257, bands of Alemanni forced the Rhine barrier while others crossed the Alps. Although the Romans were able to defeat this tribe, by 276 the dam had burst and Gaul was again brought to her knees. There were no garrisons or fortresses, and the invaders sacked, burned, and killed at will. All but a few Roman towns were completely destroyed. After this first wave of invasions, they abruptly ceased. Rome still stood, and Gaul was able to work at rebuilding once again. The Germans began to cultivate the soil alongside the Gauls, and lived under Roman law, but marriage between Germans and Gauls was forbidden.

Gaul remained relatively peaceful until the beginning of the fifth century, when barbarians again broke the Roman barriers. Compared to this second series of invasions, the flood of the first was a mere trickle. For the next century Teutonic tribes poured into Gaul, established themselves there, and eventually destroyed Rome and her empire. It was in this century that Celts whose ancestors had fled from Gaul to Britain to escape the Roman sword returned to what is now Brittany to escape the Germans who invaded Britain. The Teutonic invaders—Franks, Burgundians, Goths, and Visigoths—lived on friendly terms with the Gallic people once they had carved out territories for themselves. When Attila and his Huns invaded Gaul, Gauls and Germans defended the land together, and for the most part these last invaders passed through Gaul.

The Franks

The Franks, who settled between the Rhine and the Meuse and in the Gallo-Roman town of Paris, were destined to play a major role in the history of the country that now bears their name. The Franks were a green-eyed, fair-haired people who depended upon hunting, stock breeding, and some agriculture for existence, and they avidly raised bees for honey (the bee was the emblem of the Franks, Capets, and Napoleon I). Extremely fond of ornamentation, the Franks adorned themselves with amulets, bracelets, rings, and necklaces. Their hair was uncut but their faces were clean shaven except for a moustache. The double-headed axe, or battle ax that became so popular in the Middle Ages was their chief weapon. Their homes and dress were similar to those of primitive Gaul, and their social organization was based on the clan, over which an all-powerful chief ruled.

Although many of the Germanic tribes arrived in Gaul as Christians, the Franks did not. However, the ability of the Christian church to fill the administrative gap left by Rome's fall is exemplified by the church's dealings with the Franks. The church was aware of the need to cement its powers to the secular realm, and the bishops of Gaul took an aggressive interest in Clovis, a ferocious, barbaric Frankish king of the Merovingian line. Clovis (Louis) was anxious to enlarge his kingdom, and the Roman church was anxious to be victorious over the Arian Christianity of most Germanic tribes. While being courted by the Roman church, Clovis married a Catholic princess and was converted in 496. His baptism was immediately followed by the baptism of 3,000 warriors, and the rest of the Frankish people soon followed this example. As a champion of the faith, Clovis marched his armies into the Arian Visigothic kingdom south of the Loire and drove the Visigoths out of Gaul and into Spain. From then on the Frankish kings and the Frankish church were the joint masters of Gaul. Clovis celebrated his victory by establishing his capital in Paris.

According to Frankish custom, Clovis's kingdom was divided among his four sons after his death. This custom would repeatedly trigger fratricidal intrigue and warfare for centuries to come. By 638 the Merovingian line had petered out into a succession of shortlived weakling kings, and the mantle of leadership went to the founder of a new line, Charles Martel, who was the manager of the royal estates.

Charles Martel fought to keep the Frankish nobles in line and to keep Gaul free of Muslim raiders from Spain. Charles's victories over the latter made him a Christian hero and the strongest man in the West, but it was left to his son Pepin to establish his line as kings of the Frankish domain. With the aid and influence of Pope Zacharias, Pepin gathered the Frankish nobles together, had himself "elected" king, and dismissed the last of the Merovingians to a monastery. Pepin thus firmly established the bond between papacy and monarchy in the concept of rule by divine right.

Pepin's son, Charlemagne, was a king of such renown that several

European monarchs since that time claim to be his descendants. Charlemagne is called the Father of Europe, for under his leadership the Frankish domain was extended to the Baltic, Russia, mid-Italy, and the Pyrenees—a vast territory in any age. Charlemagne was crowned emperor, after Roman custom, on Christmas Day, 800, in St. Peter's. Pope Leo III placed the crown on Charlemagne's head, then prostrated himself before Charlemagne, a gesture which had previously been reserved for the emperor of Byzantium. This coronation marked the break between the Eastern Christian empire and the new one of the West.

Charlemagne was a just ruler and an avid reformer. Where he could not personally rule, he governed through men bound to him by ties of personal loyalty. He enforced honesty, simplified legal codes, discouraged profiteering, protected merchants, and revived educational systems. Under Charlemagne's guidance, Christianity and literacy spread, art flourished, libraries to preserve the works of antiquity were established, and architecture and building were zealously fostered.

Unfortunately, after Charlemagne's death there was no man able enough to replace him, and his empire was fragmented. From the fragments arose a host of nation states, and feudalism was born. At the bottom of the feudal ladder were the serfs, who owned little and were bound by their birth to land they cultivated for their lords. At the top of the ladder were the kings and popes, who answered only to God. In between were numerous vassals and clergy, bound to those above and below them by complex ties of fealty. The marauding of the Vikings, combined with the Muslim threat from Spain, gave the people good reason to exchange most of their freedom for a promise of protection by those who could afford weapons, horses, armor, and the support of knights.

France was then divided into countless feudal lordships, each disputing with another. In the walled town of Carcassonne the spirit of the Middle Ages comes alive even now. It is not difficult to imagine the life of the French of those centuries clinging together in relatively small groups for mutual aid and protection under the watchful guidance of the church and a feudal lord.

By the tenth century, the kings of the Carolingian line had become consistently feeble; however, one of the last Carolingian kings, Charles the Simple, took a wise gamble. Hoping to reduce the frequent destructive raids of the Norsemen, Charles chose a Nordic chieftain, Rollo, and gave him large tracts of land at the mouth of the Seine. In return, Rollo accepted Christianity and vassalage to the Frankish kings. The idea worked, and Viking raids on the French coast ceased. Rollo and his line transformed his territory into Normandy, where French would be spoken and French traditions retained. (Duke William of Normandy, five generations removed from Rollo, became the conqueror of England, thus entangling the politics of France and England, for this conquest made the king of England a vassal to the king of France.)

In 987 Hugh Capet, duke of Francia, was elected to the kingship, thereby establishing the Capetian dynasty which lasted for 300 years. The Capetian kings struggled to establish a solid base of power from which a monarch could prove effective over all of France. This meant establishing clear authority over thousands of noble vassals in times of peace as well as war. The means used was the tribunal or court. By increasing its powers and demanding that noble vassals obey its summons, the royal court of justice was able to take a more commanding attitude.

France Emerges as a Nation

Under Philip Augustus, France emerged as a nation in the thirteenth century. Through marriage, conquest, and confiscation, Philip increased his Frankish realm from the narrow strip of territory between Paris and Orléans, known as the Île-de-France, extending it from Cherbourg to the Pyrenees. He added to the meager treasury, paved the muddy streets of Paris, built the Louvre as a fortress to guard the Seine, established the University of Paris, and hastened the completion of Notre Dame.

The centralization begun by Philip continued under Louis IX, Saint Louis. Louis was a man of contrasts; he devoted much of his time to the care of the weak, disabled, and infirmed, spent hours at prayer, and built the Sainte-Chapelle, yet he brought the clergy under civil jurisdiction. By the end of his reign no part of the kingdom was without some tie to the royal government, and loyalty and respect for Louis strengthened the institution of monarchy. Before his death Louis personally led two crusades, the last of a series of attempts to drive the Muslims from the Holy Land, which is also sacred to Islam.

France played an active role in the Crusades from the first, including the pathetic Children's Crusade, when 30,000 French children unwittingly marched into slavery. The Crusades were beneficial only in that they opened new trade routes and established trade with the East.

Louis IX's successor, Philip IV, the Fair, created a general assembly of nobles, clergy, and commoners, and the Estates-General first met in 1302. Philip the Fair was the first monarch to struggle with the papacy for absolute power. This struggle led to the "Babylonian Captivity" of the papacy, when for seventy-two years the popes (who were French) resided in Avignon instead of Rome.

When Philip IV's youngest son died, the direct Capetian line also died and the throne went to Philip VI, a cousin and member of the house of Valois. However, Edward III of England, who was a grandson of Philip the Fair, laid claim to the French throne. He personally headed an invasion force into Normandy and began the Hundred Years' War.

Added to the destruction of the war—and destruction was widespread since brutish mercenaries did most of the fighting for both sides—was a new calamity: the Black Death. The bubonic plague was transmitted to Europe by the Mongol hordes that swept out of Asia and customarily catapulted their corpses over the walls of besieged cities. The Black Death, so-called because of the dark skin blotches that indicated infection, dispatched its victims within three days, during which time they spat blood, became delirious, and broke out in boils and lumps the size of eggs. Famine followed the plague, not only because crops were destroyed by war but because in many places there was no one left to cultivate the soil. Social unrest followed, and furious peasant uprisings occurred.

By 1422 the French government was in disarray and the way seemed clear for an English conquest, especially since the French throne had no legitimate heir. It was then that Joan of Arc took her place on the French stage and altered history. She convinced Charles, the disinherited son of Charles VI and the grandson of Philip VI, of her divine mission and of his right to the French throne. With her inspiration the French soldiers routed the English from the besieged city of Orléans. Soon after, Charles was crowned Charles VII in Rheims Cathedral and Joan was captured by the Burgundians, allies of the English, and burned at the stake. Filled with the memory of Joan's courage, the French drove the English from all French soil but Calais, and in 1453 the Hundred Years' War was over.

The sixteenth century saw the further consolidation of the monarchy. The concept of a strong monarchy was supported by the growing numbers of bourgeois who stood to profit by nationwide economic regulations and freedom from feudal obligations. But consolidation was interrupted by the religious wars that resulted from the Protestant Reformation.

Open warfare erupted between factions of French Huguenots and Catholics when Henry of Navarre, a Huguenot leader, was named legitimate heir to the French throne upon the extinction of the house of Valois. Henry averted civil war by formally adopting Catholicism and guaranteeing Huguenots full civil rights and freedom of public worship. Henry and his chief minister, Sully, also instituted a series of economic reforms that developed France into Europe's agricultural leader and increased its trade and industry.

Henry's son, Louis XIII, ascended the throne as a minor, and Cardinal Richelieu held the power as the chief minister. Richelieu established a civil service, under the direct control of the crown, to replace the territorial administration of the provinces by the nobles. He also began the development of a professional army, which took the raising and control of armies out of the hands of local nobility. He "exercised" his army by throwing France into the Thirty Years' War, and guided the construction of a French navy and encouraged overseas expansion. Through crown-controlled charter companies, Richelieu hoped to control Canada and claim all of the American coastline. French companies colonized the West Indies, Guiana, the East Indies, the Malay Archipelago, and Africa's west coast. Richelieu died in 1642 and Louis XIII in the following year; Louis XIV was only five years old, and Cardinal Mazarin succceeded Richelieu. Mazarin continued Richelieu's consolidation policies and suppressed attempts at rebellion by the discontented nobility. When Mazarin died, Louis was twenty-four.

Louis XIV

Louis XIV was the absolute authority in France and a prominent figure in Europe. During his reign the French domain was enlarged, the style of his court was imitated by monarchs from England to Russia, French became the international language of diplomacy, and the French dominated the arts and letters of the age. Louis was thought to be a ruler of such greatness and brilliance that he was called the Sun King. With his guidance, the Great Lakes, Mississippi River, and Mississippi delta were explored and claimed for France, and the region received the name Louisiana.

Under Louis' ministers, Le Tellier and Louvois, the French army became an impressive military machine. Louis used this army to intimidate France's neighbors and to wage expensive "wars of glory." Colbert, Louis' financial minister, who had the problem of raising sufficient funds to support the army's vast establishment, operated his economic machinery according to mercantilism, selling to other nations more than one buys. Roads were improved, canals were built, and the economy was regulated down to the smallest detail.

Louis became intoxicated by his greatness and fancied himself the center of French life. When he could no longer bear to live among the common people in Paris, he remodeled the palace at Versailles and moved his court there. Versailles was originally a humble hunting lodge, but when Louis was finished the course of a river had been diverted just to operate its fountains. The palace has miles of corridors and is so vast that it housed a court for which 500 servants prepared and served food.

Louis' love of personal luxury was also on a grand scale, and he once spent $25 million for a diamond-encrusted robe. When he was not involved in kingly business, he fervently pursued pleasure in its many forms. Louis surrounded himself with nobles who indulged his whims and would not tolerate any form of opposition or public criticism. The Huguenots were forced to convert to Catholicism or leave France; the Estates-General was never summoned; and the centralized system of Richelieu and Mazarin was carried to its logical conclusion: all municipal liberties were abolished. *"L'état,"* said Louis, *"c'est moi."*

Louis XV took his great-grandfather's throne as a minor, inheriting an increasingly corrupt nobility (which was stripped of its responsibilities but not of its wealth and privileges), a near-bankrupt treasury, and Versailles. It was Versailles and the court life there that received most of Louis XV's attention. Louis kept the governmental machinery of the Sun King in working order but replaced civil servants with corrupt and inept nobles. When a parliament of the people attempted to establish itself in order to regulate the king's actions, Louis forbade such parliaments. Though able to guess the inevitable outcome of his policies, he felt powerless to correct them. He expressed his attitude as *"Après moi, le déluge."*

While eighteenth-century France saw the aristocratic and intellectual forms of life reach their highest development, that century also saw the growing discontent of the peasants and middle class. The common people had no representation in government, were forced to carry the whole tax burden, and were disgusted by the corrupt lives of the nobility. Rousseau gave the beliefs and ideals of the common man shape and voice. He expressed an emotional approach to social problems, emphasized the individual's rights, and scorned rules and conventions. The revolution and the political order created by the Americans provided the French with a model, and the French Revolution was on its way. It might have been averted by those in power, but Louis XVI and the nobility failed to understand the problem. To their limited understanding—and they were correct—the French commoner was far better off than his counterpart in any other European country. Even Marie Antoinette's reply of "Let them eat cake" to cries for bread from Paris mobs was not meant as a cruel remark.

The Third Estate

Unwittingly, the nobles themselves opened the door for revolution. By 1788 Louis XVI's treasury was in such difficulty that the king was unable to pay his debts without a reform of the tax system that required the upper class to share the tax burden. The nobility refused to cooperate with the king's demands and, since all army officers were nobles, he could not even try to use force. The king had to yield and call a meeting of the Estates-General, which was controlled by the nobility. The nobility saw this as a chance to press for a system in which the king would govern with the advice and consent of an assembly under their domination. But when the Estates-General met in May 1789, the nobility was not prepared for the power of the Third Estate, which represented the common people. The Third Estate foiled the nobles and their allies, the clergy; declared itself the national assembly; and planned a total revision of the government.

Meanwhile, disorders erupted throughout the kingdom due to a bad harvest and the government's inability to aid the people's distress. Peasants burned manor houses and riots flared in some industrial cities. Afraid the rest of the nation would turn on Paris, members of the Third Estate in Paris began to arm themselves. On July 14 a mob, led by Danton, stormed the Bastille, murdered the mayor, and set up a new municipal government. As the wealthy began to flee the country, there was no check on the Third Estate. The assembly adopted the Declaration of the Rights of Man and the Citizen in August, abolishing all class privileges and the manorial system and instituting a representative government. The assembly then fell into dispute over the constitution.

After two years the assembly was unable to produce a suitable constitution and succeeded only in totally alienating the clergy by making all bishops and priests salaried servants of the state. Matters were further complicated by the threatened intervention of other European nations in defense of the monarchy. The Girondists, a radical faction of the assembly, forced Louis XVI, now merely a figurehead, to declare war on Austria in hopes that a war would increase revolutionary fervor throughout France. Radicals then called for a new constitution drafted by a national convention elected by universal male suffrage. In Paris, hundreds of royalist sympathizers were massacred.

When the convention met, the Girondists found themselves to be the conservatives, for the Jacobin faction was even more to the radical left. The convention abolished the monarchy, proclaimed the First French Republic, and charged the king with treason. Louis went to the guillotine in January 1793. There followed the execution of the royal family and all who opposed the Jacobins, including the Girondists. The Committee of Public Safety, headed by Robespierre, was established by the Jacobins to find and guillotine anyone who opposed the revolution in any way. In the Reign of Terror that followed, even Danton was executed. Conservative reaction then set in, and the blood bath ended with the execution of Robespierre. When the new government of directors took office in 1795, it was composed of mediocre and selfish men who repeated the experience of the old order.

Napoleon Gains Control

Napoleon Bonaparte, a young, ambitious general, saw this confusion as an opportunity to realize his dreams. After his victory in Italy, he was called a hero by the French. Napoleon, who understood human nature, was able to inspire fierce loyalty and to use the frailties of opponents to his advantage. Napoleon's brother Lucien was the president of one legislative house; and with his help, and the aid of the leading director, Napoleon carried out a coup d'état and became "first consul" of the French Republic.

Napoleon's first job was preserving the essential gains of the revolution. He established a state-controlled educational system for all levels, from the primary to the university level. The Code Napoleon was the result of his desire to develop a clear, logical, enlightened legal code. Bonaparte also ended the revolution's long quarrel with the church with a concordat which gave the civil government the right to nominate bishops and pay their salaries but allowed the church the right of their investiture and the appointment of priests. Talleyrand, who was appointed foreign minister, proved to be one of the ablest diplomats of all times. Bonaparte added to the beauties of Paris, and had further plans for the city, but was never able to carry them out.

France was now involved in wars on all sides, and once Napoleon had assured France a relative amount of "liberty, equality, and fraternity"(the revolution's slogan), these wars took a new turn. France became the offensive party, and Napoleon envisioned an empire equal to Charlemagne's. Victorious in his battles, Bonaparte was crowned Napoleon I, Emperor of the Holy Roman Empire, by Pope Pius VII in 1804. By 1812, and by direct conquest, alliances, or the placing of his brothers, sister, or friends on the various thrones, Napoleon was master of all Europe except England, which he sought to subdue by an economic embargo. Czar Alexander of Russia could not abide by this, however, as he needed England's markets for Russian grain. When Alexander refused to comply with Napoleon's wishes, Napoleon prepared for war with Russia. His march on Moscow, its capture and burning, and Napoleon's subsequent winter retreat have become almost legendary. The French army was in shreds when it marched back into Paris.

Napoleon abdicated and was exiled to the island of Elba; however, he was not finished. He escaped from Elba, raised a large army, and marched to meet the allied commander, Wellington, and his armies at Waterloo. After this defeat, Napoleon was exiled to the island of St. Helena in the South Atlantic, where he died.

The Bourbons were restored, and Louis XVIII ordered the murder of those who were loyal to Bonaparte. Louis' brother, Charles X, displeased the people by entering into a close alliance with the church, and further annoyed them by altering electoral qualifications in favor of the rich and by censoring the press. Riots resulted, and Charles fled to England.

The Bourgeois King

The next monarch was the Duke of Orléans, who had been sympathetic to the revolution. As Louis Philippe, the Bourgeois king, he made a special effort to look and act more like a town mayor than a king. During his reign the seeds of modern socialism were planted, and France had her second birth as a colonizing power; Algeria, Tunisia, and Morocco were added to the realm. Discontent was fostered among the lower classes by poor working conditions, the lack of electoral reform, and the vanished glories of Napoleon's empire. Sparked by a government ban of a banquet to promote reform, the bloody three-day February Revolution took place, and Louis Philippe fled to England.

In 1848 the national assembly was elected by universal suffrage, the Second Republic was organized, and elections for president of the republic were held. Prince Louis Napoleon, nephew of Bonaparte, was elected by an overwhelming majority, and four years later he proclaimed himself Emperor Napoleon III. A benevolent despot who sincerely had the people's interest at heart, he improved working conditions, assisted agricultural improvement, provided public housing, arbitrated labor disputes, looked after public health, and actively supported the industrial revolution in its beginnings. The city of Paris was made into the work of art it is today; the Suez Canal was completed; and protectorates were secured over Cambodia and Indochina. Nonetheless, Napoleon III failed to bring the French the glories of the first Napoleon. The war with Prussia in 1870 was his last effort to gain popularity. With France's defeat, the Third Republic was born and Napoleon was exiled.

Instead of clearly defined political parties, Third Republic France had a large number of loosely organized factions, which made positive actions difficult. The Third Republic was frequently shaken by domestic crises, but none so divided France and gained international notice as the Dreyfus case. This case provided an opportunity for the various political and religious factions to display their animosities. In the fall of 1894, Captain Alfred Dreyfus, a Jew, was accused of treason for betraying military secrets to the Germans and condemned to life imprisonment despite the fact that evidence against him was contradictory. Some was later proved to have been falsified.

It took twelve years before Dreyfus was fully cleared of guilt, and the case had become a rallying point for liberal intellectuals. The result was a political shift from moderate to radical republicanism. The energies of the radicals in power were directed against the Catholic church. Religious instruction was abolished in all state schools and members of the clergy were not permitted to teach in either state or private schools. The Act of Separation of Churches and the State was enacted, and no religion was recognized or supported by the state.

Since the time of Napeoleon the newly emerged nations of Europe had struggled to maintain a balance of power and to define clear boundaries between nations. European alliances began to resemble a kaleidoscope, with nations tumbling into new positions of alignment every generation. Overseas imperialism only complicated matters, and war was the inevitable result. The pretext for World War I was the assassination of the Austrian heir which Austria used as an excuse for the conquest of Serbia, but Russia could not permit the southern Slavs to lose their independence. France was allied to Russia, England to France, and so on. The most destructive battles of the war were fought in France; her richest areas were devastated, her most valuable industries were ruined, and she lost more men than any other country. As a partial reward for her efforts, France was awarded Alsace-Lorraine, a region contested between France and Germany since the barbarian invasions.

At first France seemed to be immune from the economic depression that plagued the world following the war. At the end of 1933, however, the Stavisky scandal, a large-scale fraud that involved several prominent deputies and a minister, became public; and the people took this as a sign of the corruption of the government. Riots rocked Paris, and France was once again divided into quarreling factions. Despite the reforms of Leon Blum, France's first Socialist premier, the Third Republic was unable to cope with the situation. It was an ailing France that followed England's lead and declared war on Hitler's Germany in 1939.

World War II

Paris soon fell and the Third Republic asked for an armistice, withdrawing from the war. In Vichy, France, which was free from direct German occupation, the senate and chamber met at a national assembly, gave dictatorial powers to Marshal Petain (who was certain of a German victory), and suspended the republic. The Vichy government agreed to pay Germany for the cost of occupation and it turned over France's raw materials and industries to German supervision. Meanwhile a young general was endearing himself to all France by organizing the forces of "Free France" from an English base. With his guidance, the French underground resistance movement organized itself. By the time British and American forces landed in French North Africa in 1942 and a provisional government of France was set up, this young general was powerful enough to be placed at the government's head. It was in this way that Charles de Gaulle began his political career.

After World War II, de Gaulle's provisional government established the Fourth Republic. Although many industries and banks were nationalized and women were granted suffrage, the constitution of the Fourth Republic was too similar to the Third's to survive for long, and de Gaulle resigned before the constitution went into effect.

The French colonial empire was severely shaken by World War II, and movements for national independence were maturing. Failing to take a movement for independence in Indochina seriously, the French sent troops to prevent what they believed would be a minor uprising. But this move convinced many of the natives that the Viet Minh ("League for Vietnamese Independence") and its leader, Ho Chi Minh, were their only salvation. Warfare broke out, and in 1954, when it became clear that France would be defeated, a conference was held in Geneva. There, nine countries, including France, agreed to a cease-fire and began the process that resulted in the division of Viet Nam. The communist states continued to support the north, and the south received American assistance.

Pierre Mendes-France, the radical prime minister who brought France out of Indochina, was determined to settle things in North Africa as well, and in 1956 both Tunisia and Morocco were granted independence. However, when the Algerians also demanded independence, trouble erupted. Algeria was not a colony or a protectorate; it was constitutionally a part of mainland France. In 1954, Algerian nationalists revolted and the French attempted to suppress them by force. In 1958, a conspiracy of settlers and army officers carried out a coup d'état, extended their rule to Corsica, and seemed to threaten France itself. The assembly voted Charles de Gaulle into office as prime minister with full power to revise the constitution. This was the end of the Fourth Republic.

The Fifth Republic

De Gaulle rewrote the constitution to give France a strong president in the hope of ensuring political stability. In December 1958, he was elected president of the Fifth Republic. The new constitution severely reduced the powers of the assembly. De Gaulle aimed to make France a great power with himself at the head.

De Gaulle, seemingly unable to hear the growing cries for reform, consistently reminded the French: "Without me, this country wouldn't be anything." For almost a decade the French believed him. Then, in May 1968, discontented workers and students banded together against Gaullism.

For nearly a month France was crippled by nationwide strikes that shut down industry and filled the streets with garbage. Riots spread through the cities. De Gaulle submitted his policies to a public vote with the promise that, if they were defeated, he would resign. His policies were approved, and de Gaulle remained in power. A year later, de Gaulle again submitted to a public referendum. This time the vote was *non,* and de Gaulle resigned. He died in November 1970.

Following de Gaulle's resignation, the Gaullist candidate, Georges Pompidou, won a run-off election against Jacques Duclos of the Communist Party. A Gaullist majority was maintained in the assembly.

In 1974, following the death of Pompidou, Valéry Giscard d'Estaing became the third president of the Fifth Republic. A conservative, Giscard d'Estaing won the election in a run-off with François Mitterrand, the leftist candidate. Seven years later, in the 1981 presidential election, socialist Mitterrand defeated Giscard d'Estaing and then won a solid majority in the National Assembly elections. In 1986, however, conservatives regained power in the National Assembly, producing an uneasy alliance between Right and Left called *cohabitation.* Mitterand won reelection in 1988, and his party gained sufficient strength in parliament for him to install a conservative Socialist premier, Michel Rocard. Amid widespread public dissent in France, French forces helped defeat Iraq in the Persian Gulf War early in 1991. In May of that year, Edith Cresson became the first woman to assume the post of premier in France. Although a traditional Socialist, she supported the government's more moderate policies. In June 1991, France agreed to sign the Nuclear Nonproliferation Treaty.

In 1992, political events in France centered on Mitterand's declining power and influence. In part because of Socialist setbacks in the by-elections of March 1992, Cresson resigned after serving only ten months.

The conservative coalition won a resounding victory in the March 1993 parliamentary elections forcing the Socialist Party to oust its leader, Laurent Fabius, and Mitterand to form a new government of *cohabitation* under Prime Minister Edouard Balladur. Balladur has successfully experimented with a tolerant, nonconfrontational approach to politics in a system traditionally operating on deep national division. At the beginning of 1994, he was seen as the leading presidential contender from his neo-Gaullist *Rassemblement pour la République (RPR)* for the presidential elections in 1995. Mitterand had already announced that he would not be a candidate. The intensity of the French government shift to the left in the 1980s seems to be waning in the 1990s.

Charles de Gaulle, the man who single-handedly saved France from civil war and founded the Fifth Republic.

French Government

Richard de Angelis

Unlike the United States, which is still a young nation, France and the French have a long history behind them when they think about politics. Throughout that history the French have always managed to survive, and often to prosper. They have drunk many times from the cup of national grandeur and have never forgotten the taste.

But French political history is also a story of troubles and violence. Having never considered the peaceful Swiss to be their ideal, France has never been either a stable or an easy country to govern. The difficulties had already begun when France was a monarchy, before the United States even existed. Since the Revolution of 1789, the French have been searching for that system of government which would give them liberty and order, peace and grandeur. Even though the search has not yet been successful, the effort is a fascinating topic to study.

The French kings of the Dark and Middle Ages were the first to encounter difficulties in the ten-century struggle (from the fall of Rome to the Renaissance) to build the French nation and develop the machinery of a powerful state. The costs of their struggle against both internal and external enemies were high. The unity of the nation, as well as the grandeur and efficiency of the state, are important parts of a heritage that also includes distrust of that state. Even today, although all Frenchmen are firmly attached to their country, many regions (such as Brittany) feel a need for greater freedom to run their own local affairs.

With the nation created and the state built up, it took several more centuries to perfect the institutions of the absolute and divine-right monarchy. The height of glory of the Sun King, Louis XIV, and Versailles lasted only a short time, however. The monarchy waged too many wars, protected too many privileges, oppressed the poor with its taxes for too long. The French wanted more than a strong and glorious leader; they wanted a fair and just one as well.

The End of Monarchy

The monarchy collapsed in the Revolution of 1789, which let loose forces that have not yet been tamed. The old order—the nobility and the monarchy—was finished, it seemed, but a new political order was still groping to be born. The bourgeoisie (middle classes) came into politics to fight for their own interests and for the rights of man. But they hadn't asked for war with nearly all the rest of Europe. They hadn't anticipated terror or conflict between the rich and poor and between Catholics and republicans within France itself. They welcomed a savior in 1799: Napoleon Bonaparte. They thought he had finally brought to a close the process of revolution.

Bonaparte consolidated the gains of the middle classes, reformed the law code, made peace with the Catholic church, and strengthened the centralized state bureaucracy. But the cup of glory overflowed in foreign wars, and the period of revolution, instability, and experimentation did not really end until 1875. Between 1799 and 1875 the French experienced the rise and fall of the First Empire, the Bourbon Restoration, the July Monarchy, the Second Republic of 1848, the Second Empire of Louis Napoleon, and the uprising of the people of Paris in the Commune of 1870 (the first workers' government in the world, which was drowned in blood after only a few weeks by conservative republicans).

In 1870, the year of the Commune and of France's defeat in war with Bismark's Germany, the empire of Louis Napoleon dissolved. Many Frenchmen anticipated that the most natural course was a return to monarchy. For five years, from 1870–1875, the seat of the king was kept warm. But the monarchists were divided among themselves over who should be king. And the rightful pretender to the throne refused to return to France unless he could bring back with him the white flag of the Bourbons to replace the tricolor flag the French had grown attached to since 1789.

In 1875, for want of anything better, the conservative Third Republic crept in by the back door—by one vote. It was said that it was the regime that divided the French the least. In fact, it managed to last more than sixty years. It weathered many attacks from opponents on the left and on the right, from socialists and from the church. It triumphed over a coalition of nobles, Catholics, and the army in the famous Dreyfus affair at the turn of the century. (Dreyfus, a Jewish army captain, was falsely accused of treason. The refusal of the conservatives to correct his unjust sentence, because it would hurt the army, was the cause of the affair.) Afterward, in 1905, the republicans successfully separated the church and the state, thus ending the subsidies paid to the church since the time of Napoleon.

But despite victory in World War I, the Third Republic could not handle the international crises caused by Nazi Germany or the domestic conflict that arose in the 1930s as a result of the worldwide depression. In 1940, in a few short weeks, the French army was catastrophically defeated by Germany. The French government abdicated its powers to the hero of World War I, the conservative Marshal Petain. The Third Republic died with few regrets.

Its successor, called simply the French State, replaced the motto of the French Revolution, "Liberty, Equality, Fraternity," with a more conservative one, "Work, Family, Fatherland." Although it was at first recognized as the legitimate government of France by the United States, its leaders were too conservative and too tainted by collaboration with the Germans to be accepted for long. But an almost unknown general, Charles de Gaulle, had refused to submit to the German victors in 1940. His forces, in alliance with the internal resistance fighters and, most importantly, with the allied armies, later swept the Vichy regime into the dustbin of history.

Return of the Republic

In 1946 the French returned to the idea of a republic, this time the Fourth Republic. They dreamt of a strong and pure republic, one that would unite them in a common spirit of progress and social reform. But the dreams were soon dashed by reality. The French economy recovered and grew with aid from the United States and under the guidance of Jean Monnet's national planning. France joined the Common Market and began to modernize her economy after nearly a century of stagnation, but her problems were too many and too difficult. It was hard for her to admit the fact that she was no longer the most important power in Europe.

To add to the humiliation of defeat in 1940, France also lost her empire: Indochina (Vietnam, Cambodia, Laos) in 1954 and North and Black Africa soon afterward. In Algeria—much like the United States in Vietnam—she did not know how to win against fighters for independence but didn't have the decisiveness to admit defeat.

To keep friendly relations with, and the protection of the United States, France also had to accept an alliance with her old foe, Germany. And the cold war between East and West destroyed the wartime progress in bringing the workers and the Communist party back into society.

Weak and unstable governments could not adequately solve these difficult problems of the Fourth Republic. The frustrated army in Algeria, seeking to keep Algeria French, took over the local government in 1958 and threatened a military takeover in France itself. Frightened by the possibility of being shot or thrown into the Seine by army paratroopers, the politicians abdicated in favor of a savior. This time it was General de Gaulle, who had been out of power since 1946, writing his memoirs and waiting silently at his country home for the right moment to return.

He returned to rule France for eleven years in a manner that is still controversial. The constitution of the Fifth Republic, which he founded, is today the law of the land, even after his departure. It is the thirteenth constitution the French have given themselves since the French Revolution. It was revised in 1962 and was almost revised again in 1969. The joke about the French bookseller who didn't have a copy of the constitution because he didn't stock periodicals is almost too true to be amusing.

Paradoxes

Even to experts, politics in France is confusing and paradoxical, but always changing and fascinating. From glory to humiliation and back, it has tried every type of politics—monarchy, empire, republic—and ended up somehow dissatisfied with them all. Despite their splendid culture and economic progress, the French have always been disappointed by their politics. Although cautious in their actions and personal lives, they have pushed all their ideas to their logical limits, so that France has often seemed both a museum for outmoded ideas and a laboratory for the newest ones.

There are paradoxes in the average Frenchman too. (Of course, there is no average Frenchman but hundreds of different types, and that is part of the problem.) He has been compared to a radish: red and revolutionary on the outside but white and conservative on the inside. In other words, he is a man with his heart on the left but his pocketbook on the right. De Gaulle, who loved France but couldn't stand the French, once said that it was impossible to govern a country that is proud of producing more than 500 different varieties of cheese. To each his own taste in cheese, to each his own ideas.

If the French are usually difficult to govern, it is largely because they don't like to be governed. Although they recognize the need for a state, its politics have as often hurt them as helped them. Politicians are seen as "they": those people who are responsible for taxes, wars, paperwork, and interference in daily life. The image of the state is often that of the petty official who doesn't care about personal problems but goes only by the book. He acts on the old French saying, "To understand everything is to forgive everything." But not wanting or able to forgive, he doesn't often try to understand.

In response, the French obey when they must, but without believing, and constantly try to get around the rules that seem to them ridiculous or unfair. An incident that happened recently to an American researcher in a small, Catholic farm village in France is symbolic of this attitude. Needing to send out a number of questionnaires to local farmers, the researcher was advised by a respected woman on the town council to make a deal with the postman to hand deliver them without stamps for five dollars, paid directly to the postman. This way the postman did the same work, got five dollars for it, and only the state was the loser.

The French know too that the regime they live under may not last. For example, an older Frenchman has already lived under three different republics and the regime of Marshal Petain. During World War II, de Gaulle was condemned to death as a traitor by Petain. After the war, Petain was imprisoned as a traitor by de Gaulle. In such circumstances, it doesn't pay to get involved too deeply in politics. Most Frenchmen have learned to wait for the winner, to "cultivate their gardens," to look out first for themselves and their families.

On the positive side, the French regularly vote in elections and to a greater extent than Americans do. Most are proud of being republicans and of being citizens of the country that produced the French Revolution and the Declaration of the Rights of Man. Jealous of their equality with each other, they hate the pretenses of superiority of the privileged or the arbitrariness of a strong ruler. When their saviors have finished their work, they have usually been discarded without praise, qualms, or regrets for fear that they might try to rule forever. No people is as devoted, at least in principle, to the defense of the rights of the individual.

Yet at the same time the French would be happy to discover a good king—or the equivalent, a great statesman—who would be an efficient and just sovereign, safeguarding their progress and prestige, their unity and tranquility. Something of a constitutional monarch, de Gaulle attempted to fill this need but did not quite succeed. The tragedy of the French is that, while they need and want a strong leader who will be just, they are still so haunted by their revolt against the old regime nearly two hundred years ago that they discourage all strong leaders for fear they will not be just and fair. Since 1789 they have swung from republic to savior and back again, a potentially tragic circus act without a net. The major problem of modern French politics is somehow to reconcile the principles of the republic (equality and liberty) with the need of the country for strong, progressive leadership.

A Lack of Consensus

The instability of politics in France is caused not only by distrust for the state but also by the fact that—although intensely proud of their nation and culture—the French are divided and opposed to each other on most political questions. There is no consensus on what politics should be like, or how conflicts should be solved, because the French Revolution created opposing groups but did not give the victory clearly to either side. To these conflicts we must add even more ancient divisions and disputes, which create distrust and a tendency to avoid the face-to-face compromises that make true self-government work. Since there are many different and conflicting groups, none gets all of what it wants. Each is usually willing to defend its "acquired rights" against change and to abdicate to the central state and its rulers the political power to deal with conflicts and to pursue reform. Strong leaders have managed to do what has had to be done despite these divisions, but no government has thus far been able to eliminate them.

Regional Differences

The oldest divisions in France are regional. The people of Avignon have not forgotten that, under the popes in the Middle Ages, they paid no taxes. The Bretons, like the Alsatians and the Basques, speak their own language—at least the older generation does at home. In some areas of the Massif Central, the repression of the Protestants before the Revolution has not been completely forgiven. In western France, on the other hand, the conservative and Catholic peasants have not forgotten that their ancestors were persecuted by the republicans in Paris during the French Revolution. In fact, the major division of the French—between those living north and those living south of the Loire River—dates back to Roman times. Even today the Frenchman of the north thinks of the southerner as lazy, loud, overly gregarious, and fickle. The southerner dismisses the northerner as a loner who is uninteresting and unable to enjoy life. De Gaulle, a northerner who was born in Lille (near Belgium) and raised in Paris, was never really popular in the sunny climes of the Midi.

Regional divisions have been overlaid with religious ones. Only about a fourth of the French attend Mass regularly in this overwhelmingly Catholic country, the "first daughter" of the church. Practicing Catholics are concentrated in Alsace-Lorraine in the east, Brittany in the west, and on the southern edge of the Massif Central, the mountainous region of central France. Entire regions of the country have been dechristianized, especially in working-class areas in the north, in the cities, and in some peasant areas in the south.

In the nineteenth century, the church became more closely associated with monarchical and conservative forces, seeking to return to its previously important position under the kings. Republicans tended to be nonpracticing, anticlerical, and even atheistic as a result. This is the major division between the left and the right in France, although new economic and social issues have split both camps into many different factions.

Since the separation between church and state in 1905, the conflict between Catholics and anticlericals has been diminishing. It is not dead, however. In the 1965 election for the presidency of the republic between de Gaulle and François Mitterrand, the candidate of the left, most practicing Catholics voted for de Gaulle and most atheists and anticlericals for Mitterrand. Ironically, although the appeal of the church has been steadily weakened among workers for many years, it has been argued that its influence is still felt indirectly—in the Communist party. The party is often seen as a new church, with its own hierarchy, rituals, priests, and promised land. This conflict of ideas makes life more interesting but also much more difficult.

Social and Economic Divisions

The most recent major division of the French has been social and economic. On the one hand are the farmers, declining in numbers very rapidly but still powerful, individualistic, and generally conservative (even when dumping potatoes in the streets to protest their declining income).

In the middle are the bourgeois, the businessmen, shopkeepers, bureaucrats, and professional men who have dominated politics since the French Revolution by elbowing out the nobles. Although divided into republicans and conservatives, they have united with the peasants to put down the demands of the workers, whom they saw as threatening society.

The workers are divided into Catholics, Socialists, Communists, and the uninvolved, but all share a sense of living in a ghetto and of not getting their fair share. Their unions are weak and divided but militant; strikes tend to be short and bitter. The workers have prospered somewhat through economic growth, but not as much as the middle classes. Largely neglected by de Gaulle, who was more interested in foreign affairs, they took their revenge in May 1968. The greatest sit-down strike in history shut France down for a month and almost forced de Gaulle out of office. The reintegration of the workers into society on an equal basis is one key problem of French internal politics.

The divisions of the French are mirrored and expressed in the number and platforms of the French parties. Keeping old issues alive beyond their time and making most conflicts worse, they have usually been unable to simplify the problems of society or give the voter a clear choice between different policies for the government to follow. Still important, despite the wishes of de Gaulle, the parties seem to have changed somewhat in recent years, but it is too soon to tell for sure.

The most controversial party in France is the French Communist party. Although smaller than the Italian Communist party, it is probably more important because of France's more strategic location in the heart of Europe. The party was founded in 1920 by a majority of the delegates to the Socialist Party Congress, bitter about the massive bloodletting of World War I (France lost more than a million men) and hopeful for the success of the new Soviet revolution in Russia. Many had not expected the new party to be as harsh as it turned out to be.

The Communist Party

The Communist party spent its first ten years in isolation, preoccupied with internal fights, but in the face of the Nazi threat—both to France and to the Soviet Union—it changed from hostility to all other parties to cooperation with the Socialists and Radicals in the Popular Front Alliance in 1936. At the same time, the Socialist and smaller Communist unions merged into one. Communist militants were the more active, especially in the newly unionized industries, and they emerged dominant in the General Confederation of Labor, France's most important labor union.

During World War II the Communists were the most dedicated, efficient, and powerful force of resistance to the occupying Germans. Although they fought for their own political ends, they also fought for patriotic reasons, and in cooperation with Socialists, Catholics, and other noncommunists.

After the war de Gaulle brought the party into the government. The head of the party, Maurice Thorez, urged his followers to lay down their arms, to cooperate with de Gaulle, and to get back to work so that France could be rebuilt. Only in 1947, after disputes between East and West had grown bitter, were the Communists temporarily forced out of the government.

Isolated in the 1950s, the Communists then tried to tone down their image to create the possibility of some cooperation again with other leftist parties. They renounced, they said, the idea of one-party rule "after the revolution" and decided to seek a peaceful, French approach to socialism. They demonstrated their independence when the Soviet Union invaded Czechoslovakia in August 1968 by publicly criticizing the Soviets for the first time in decades.

The Communist party's influence in France remained strong in the 1960s and 1970s. Through control of the General Confederation of Labor, the party exerted great influence on the economy (as it showed in May 1968) by shutting off electricity, water, transportation, and other large industries when workers' interests were not taken sufficiently into account. Although doubt grew that the French Communists still believed in real revolution, they constantly pushed for social reform. Through the local governments the party controlled and with a significant number of seats in the National Assembly, the party was credited with doing much to improve the lives of workers.

The party's electoral strength for many years after World War II ran between one-fifth and one-fouth of the voters, enough to make itself felt by all and to dominate any left coalition bent on reform. However, while the 1981 elections saw France's government shift to the left, there was decreased support for the Communists. François Mitterrand, the Socialist candidate and an outspoken critic of the Communists, won the presidency in a run-off election against Giscard d'Estaing, and he won a solid Socialist majority in the National Assembly elections that followed. With only sixteen percent of the total vote, the Communists were left with only 43 of 491 seats in the National Assembly, a loss of more than 40.

The French Communist party, left with a seemingly marginal role, still has a significant number of members, most active in places where large numbers of workers live. It has its own newspaper, *l'Humanité,* and it controls a publishing company, party schools, sports clubs, and vacation spots. Its future, however, remains uncertain. The majority of French voters, while shifting to the left in the 1981 elections, clearly stated that it was the Socialists, not the Communists, who should be given the chance to guide France through the 1980s.

The Socialists

The French Socialist party is older than the Communist party by fifteen years. In fact, its full name, French Section of the Workers'

International, dates from 1905. During its earliest years, the party was torn between Marxist and revolutionary ideas and its reformist and electoral practices.

During the First World War the Socialists participated in the "government of national union" that led France to victory, although they had promised before the war that they would never help the capitalists of their own country fight against the workers of another. A split in 1920 hurt the party so badly that it took a decade to recover, and it constantly worried about the new Communist party on its left. In 1936, the victory at the polls of the Popular Front led to a Socialist prime minister, Leon Blum. As in Roosevelt's New Deal, this government introduced collective bargaining, higher wages, shorter hours, social security, and paid vacations for workers. But it failed to bring France together in a time of international crises.

Active during the resistance period, the Socialists took part in the government after World War II and helped introduce further social reforms such as the nationalization of coal mines, insurance companies, some banks, and the Renault automobile factories. However, the party of the postwar years failed to attract new blood. It took a hard line against the Communists during the cold war and participated in many of the middle-of-the-road governments of the Fourth Republic, often as a prisoner of the more conservative parties with which it had to work. It thus managed to lose support on the left while failing to gain much support on the right, and it split internally on almost all major issues. The Socialists supported the return of de Gaulle to power in 1958, a decision which caused a significant minority to quit the party to found a small, new, more purely socialist party. But soon the Socialists returned to the opposition, joining the Communists, criticizing de Gaulle's increasingly personal use of his tremendous powers.

The French Socialist party of the 1960s and early 1970s had fewer members than the Communists. They were active primarily in the north (near Belgium) and in the south (around Marseilles), and the party was strongest among minor civil servants. Its electoral strength hovered around fifteen percent of the voters. During this period the party tried to form a loose alliance with the Communists and other leftist groups.

The Socialist party's position in France changed seemingly overnight in the presidential elections of 1981. The voters, apparently dissatisfied with their conservative government but increasingly wary of the Communist party platform, turned to the Socialists for change. Taking advantage of disorganization in the coalition government of Valéry Giscard d'Estaing, the Socialist candidate, François Mitterrand, scored a surprise victory in a run-off with Giscard d'Estaing. His goal of sixteen years, to be president of France, had finally been met. His party then won 290 of 491 National Assembly seats, further strengthening his position.

Mitterrand's support came from a broad sector of French society, but was unquestionably influenced by social changes taking place in France: increasing urbanization, inflation, unemployment, and the increase in the number of women in the labor force. His outspoken criticism of the Communists may have encouraged more conservative voters to give him a chance.

Mitterrand promised to make some sweeping economic and social changes. Almost immediately after taking office he announced an increase in the minimum wage and increased financial aid to the poor. He vowed to give low-interest loans to small businesses to help get the economy moving again. He immediately began working to create new jobs for the unemployed, particularly the young. Mitterrand also said that he wanted to shorten the work week and increase workers' paid vacation to five weeks. Perhaps his most controversial campaign promise was to nationalize certain key industries, but as his term began it was still uncertain how he would proceed.

The Center Parties

With the Socialists in power and the Communists in disarray, the center parties have been divided and weak. Most of these groups have no real party organization, no way of disciplining their deputies to vote the same way, and few members in the country at large. The names of these various groups—Independents, Moderates, Peasants, Republicans—have changed so often that it is difficult to follow their recent histories. The Christian Democrats, still strong in Italy and Germany and one of the most important parties of the Fourth Republic, have virtually no members left in France. The Independents have split into those who joined the Gaullists and those who remain faithful to their name and independent of the Gaullists. With the Socialists in power, these center parties may try to reorganize to move France back to the center, but some of them may dissolve into the change.

The Gaullist Party

A relatively new party, but one with great stength for many years, the Gaullist party grew as de Gaulle's power grew. The biggest surprise to everyone during the Fifth Republic was the emergence of such a strong Gaullist party with a majority in the National Assembly. It was the first time in French history that one party consistently had so much support.

It is difficult to describe the Gaullist party because what gave it unity was not a set of ideas so much as loyalty to one man, de Gaulle, and the domination of a small band of his "companions" who ruled in his place.

(De Gaulle did not want to be tied to any one party, so that he could be free and above them all.) Within the party have coexisted "Gaullists of the left," who saw de Gaulle as the one man capable of introducing overdue social reforms; "state Gaullists," who wanted to strengthen the grandeur and prestige of France and the government; and "conservative Gaullists" (like Georges Pompidou, the second president of the republic), who were pro-American and interested in building a French version of the British Conservative party. The bulk of the rank-and-file members and deputies were called simply de Gaulle's "foot soldiers," who were expected to stay in line and do what they were told.

Although most observers felt that the party would disintegrate with de Gaulle gone (in the same way a previous Gaullist party collapsed in the 1950s), this did not take place. However, with the 1981 election, the Gaullists found themselves struggling to reorganize and seek out new support.

The traditional parties dominated political life during the Fourth Republic meeting in a national assembly building in Paris that was literally a "house without windows." Many Frenchmen felt that the deputies were more concerned with their own political moves inside than with the real problems of a changing France they could not see outside. But the real problem was not so much with the institutions of the republic as with the voters themselves, who continued to vote for many different and often anti-republican parties, and with the scope of the problems the politicians had to face.

In January of 1946, General de Gaulle resigned. Later that year, the constitution of the Fourth Republic was accepted by a majority of the voters in a referendum, but not very enthusiastically. Contrary to the wishes of de Gaulle, the new constitution gave power primarily to the legislature. In 1947, de Gaulle formed a short-lived political party, the Rally of the French People, to push for a strong executive (and to fight communism).

Instead of being a strong executive, the President of the Republic (elected for seven years by the two houses of the legislature, the National Assembly and the Council of the Republic) was only a figurehead, much like the British queen. The more important prime minister and his cabinet, who were responsible to parliament, had to get a majority of the deputies to agree to support them. The prime minister could not, in practice, easily dissolve the legislature by calling for new elections, and he had few other means of persuading or forcing the deputies to do what had to be done in order to keep the country running. The legislature, however, could censure the government, both formally and informally, fairly easily. It could debate whatever bills it, or the powerful legislative committees wanted to debate, regardless of the wishes of the government.

This system could have been made to work if France had had a strong two-party system. (A very similar system works well in England, where the majority party controls both the executive and the legislature and can work out its problems in meetings within the party.) But a strong *two*-party system was the one thing the Fourth Republic did not have.

The electoral system in use at the time was supposed to be the fairest type of proportional representation. Theoretically, if a party won 30 percent of the votes it also received 30 percent of the seats. (In the United States it is winner-take-all, even if the victory is won by only 51 percent.) The French system had the unfortunate disadvantage of preserving small and extremist parties that would otherwise have been eliminated.

During most of the Fourth Republic, the Communists (for example) received a quarter of the total votes. On the extreme right, other groups received smaller percentages but still won important numbers of votes, and seats as well. Thus the number of deputies left in the middle to form a government was abnormally small. Since, moreover, no single party could get a majority of the votes, all governments had to be coalitions (made up of different parties). They had to get along even though they were usually opposed to each other in their ideas and goals. To make matters even worse, new and difficult problems of decolonization, German rearmament, and especially the war in Algeria nearly split all the parties down the middle.

Most of the time the result was cabinet instability, a different government every seven months, and the politics of "immobilism"—waiting for things to happen rather than trying to influence them in advance. (The major exception was the government of Pierre Mendes-France in 1954, which ended the war in Indochina.) The ultimate result was that the French became disillusioned and disgusted. When the threat of a political coup came from the army, no one was willing to defend the republic, which did not and could not defend itself.

The New Constitution

The new constitution of the Fifth Republic was largely the handiwork of de Gaulle and his followers. Some concessions had to be made to the parties that supported de Gaulle's return, however. Thus the prime minister still had to get a majority in the National Assembly, as under the Fourth Republic, and could be censured by a majority of the deputies. The president of the republic, until 1962, was indirectly elected for seven years by an electoral college—made up of local town-council members and mayors, in addition to the national deputies. Only in 1962 did de Gaulle submit (unconstitutionally) a referendum to the French people providing for direct election of the president by the people themselves. But de Gaulle got what he wanted in the constitution: a strong president and a weak legislature—his goals since 1946. The constitution was approved by almost 80 percent of the voters in September 1958. The general, who once said he did not become chief of state to inaugurate chysthanemum expositions, could be well pleased with himself.

The president that the voters approved would have broader powers in many respects than even the president of the United States. Elected for seven years, he cannot be removed, except for high treason. He is commander in chief of the armed forces. He presides over the cabinet of ministers, negotiates and ratifies treaties, signs or delays bills, and receives ambassadors. He chooses the prime minister, who is then responsible to the legislature. He can dissolve the assembly and call for new elections as he wishes, a power no American president has had.

In addition, the French president can present issues to the people by referendum (a power de Gaulle often tended to abuse) and he can take any measures he decides are necessary in a time of grave national emergency. These two powers are ideas of de Gaulle himself. The power of referendum gives him a means to go directly to the people without going through the parties or parliament. The power to take measures to safeguard the state and the nation in a crisis is the result of de Gaulle's personal experience in the crisis of 1940, when no one seemed to know who was really in charge of the country. It is this power, which de Gaulle used to combat insurrections in the army and rightist assassination attemps, which most worries many Frenchmen. In the hands of an unscrupulous president, the republic could be subverted legally from within. The referendum is also controversial because the answer the people give depends largely on who gets to write the question. In the past, the Bonapartes, like de Gaulle, used the referendum to get a vote of confidence from the people to continue to rule just as they pleased. The French may have good reason for believing that other Frenchmen cannot be trusted for long with so much power. In reacting against the weakness of the Fourth Republic, the Fifth Republic may have gone too far the other way.

The reaction against the Fourth Republic can also be seen in the limited role of the legislature in the new constitution. The National Assembly, of 481 members, is elected for five years directly by the people. The Senate, of 273 members, is elected indirectly, and for nine years, by local officials and the national deputies, one-third every three years. Instead of utilizing proportional representation, the new system is more like the American system, but with two ballots. On the first Sunday of an election, only those with a majority win—usually only a small number. On the second Sunday, there is a runoff, and the persons with the most votes (not necessarily a majority) win. This system favors the strongest and most moderate parties.

Only the National Assembly can censure the government, but the Senate has the power to delay bills if it wants. Both houses meet for six months during the year, once in the fall and once in the spring.

The government can now force the legislature to cooperate, even if it doesn't want to; it tells the deputies which bills to consider and in what order. If the government decides to ask for a "blocked vote," the assembly must vote on the government version of any bill *without* amendments, unless accepted by the government. The budget must be approved or rejected within seventy days; after that time it goes into effect automatically.

In order to discourage deputies from voting against a government just so they can have a chance to be ministers in the next, all ministers must have resigned their seats in parliament. If the government falls, they have nowhere to go back to, as they had before. In order to bring down a government by censuring it, over half the deputies must vote to do so; abstentions are counted as votes for the government. Thus even if a government does not have a positive majority, it can continue if there is no negative majority against it. The government can pose the question of confidence on any bill, so that if it is defeated it must resign. Unless the government is censured, the bill then goes into effect. Thus bills can become law simply because no one wants to cause a crisis by opposing them, even if there is not otherwise a majority for them.

These measures, plus the fact that the Gaullists for many years had a majority in the National Assembly (but not in the Senate), weakened the legislature a great deal—as de Gaulle had hoped.

The Centralized State

The key difference between the United States and France is that discontent has tended to bypass the powerless assembly and take the form either of secret lobbying in the bureaucracy or violent street demonstrations. Practically every group in French society—workers, students, the army, peasants, shopkeepers—has resorted to violent strikes, demonstrations, or worse to try to force its will on what it has considered an unheeding state and an increasingly autocratic president.

Unlike the presidency and the legislature, the civil service and the institutions of local government have not been drastically changed under the new republic, but only reformed to bring them into line with an industrial and mobile society. They still provide the machinery that keeps the nation going despite its political troubles.

France is a centralized state while the United States is a federation of states that largely govern themselves. Begun under the medieval kings as a way of creating national unity against rebellious provinces, the centralized state was perfected by Napoleon, and hasn't changed much since. Under Napoleon's school system, it was said that at any hour of the day all the schoolchildren in a given grade were looking ot the same book and learning the same lesson. Even today, a mayor who wants to build a swimming pool has to have approval (and money) from Paris, and this can take months if not years. Centralization was necessary to fight the enemies of the republic, it was thought after the revolution, but it was continued also because of the French desire for equal treatment. The French would probably be scandalized by the disparities in allowances for schools or poverty programs that exist in the United States.

The decisions of the state are enforced through the central Ministry of the Interior. In the United States, the Department of the Interior handles forests and the like, but in France this ministry handles most of the police in the country. (Towns and cities do have local police forces, in addition to the national police force.) This ministry also runs elections, takes the census, and—most importantly—controls the prefects.

The revolution of 1789 wiped out the old provincial boundaries and set up a new system of communes (towns and villages), cantons, arrondissements, and departments (roughly like large American counties). Of the 36,000 communes, many are too small to be self-sufficient. Even many of the 90 or so departments are too small to be of much importance in dealing with economic and social problems. On both levels there has recently been consolidation to make government more efficient.

To the head of each department the central government appoints a prefect. He is a civil servant who sees that the laws are obeyed, that the decisions of the government are enforced, and that the state is not subverted. They are frequently rotated from department to department to keep them loyal only to the central government, and they have been replaced by every new regime. Their role is extremely powerful, although they have to try to get along with the local inhabitants.

The prefects are "assisted" by departmental councils, which are elected. They have very little influence, however, and serve mainly to give politicians a chance to become known.

At lower levels, mayors and town councilmen have important political influence, and translate the will of their localities into governing decisions, but the scope of their powers is limited. Communes are not free to tax themselves as they wish; instead, they are dependent on the central government for money and for loans. The mayors draw up the budgets and are considered agents of the state, responsible for keeping records and the like. If they fail to do so, they can be removed. Although local government is honest, close to the people, and responsible for many improvements, the scope for experimental and truly new ideas is almost nonexistent. However, what is lost in local self-government is perhaps gained in greater uniformity in the enforcement of the laws in the entire nation. It is less possible—or likely—in France for an entire region to defy the legitimate laws of the land the way some elected officials and police have been able to do for so long in some parts of America.

The civil service in France is also different from that in the United States. In France, many workers could be considered as employed by the government because they work for nationalized industries, such as gas, electricity, mines, insurance, or railroads. Teachers and professors are also on the govermnent payroll. These types of government employees, however, act very much like private employees. Since 1946 they have even had the right to strike, which American civil servants do not, and have often used that right. At the upper levels is the small group of bureaucrats, who emerge from stiff competitive examinations. They come largely from the upper classes, but they have a rigorous education and strong sense of dedication to the state and the public good. It is this group (hardly representative of ordinary Frenchmen) that has made the economy grow in a planned manner since the end of the war. Under de Gaulle, many civil servants even became ministers, whereupon opponents cried that the government was a technocracy run by experts who knew little about people.

In France today, the economy is growing and modernizing itself, and the stability and prestige of the government have increased. With de Gaulle the French became more independent, more confident, and more concerned with helping underdeveloped nations than with clinging to dreams of empire. De Gaulle ended the war in Algeria, tamed the rebellious army, and gave pride to a people suffering from bitter humiliations. He cleared the way for the French to pursue solutions to their domestic problems. He provided for the election of the president by the people and for the first majority party in French history.

But the negative side of his regime is also important. Economic change did not benefit all Frenchmen equally. His foreign policy often managed only to alienate his friends without winning over his enemies. His preoccupation with foreign affairs meant neglect of the desires of most

Frenchmen, who cared more about hospitals, schools, and highways than a French atomic bomb. De Gaulle became a symbol of arrogance and arbitrary rule for many of his countrymen.

In May 1968 the faults of the regime almost spoiled its claim of being a strong regime that brought peace and order. An alternating policy of weakness and repression magnified student and worker discontent, and as a result paralyzed the country for a month. De Gaulle's first reaction to these momentous events was contemptuous. But eventually, he realized that the French had to be listened to and wanted to participate more in their own government.

His last year was spent in pushing through student and worker reforms. But his efforts were blocked by his conservative friends and hampered by his authoritarian personality. His final proposal for a referendum, to bring government closer to the people, failed to win a majority in the spring of 1969. He resigned following that defeat. Georges Pompidou, an intelligent, crafty Gaullist and former prime minister, was then elected to be the new president.

Pompidou died in 1974, and Valéry Giscard d'Estaing became the new president, governing with a coalition of Gaullist and centrist forces. In 1981, however, the French decided it was time for a major change. Concerned with rising inflation and unemployment, they elected Socialist François Mitterrand as their new president and then gave him a majority in the National Assembly.

After his election to the Elysée, President Mitterrand pushed for a number of reforms touching virtually all aspects of French society. Mitterrand nationalized several large financial and industrial groups and called for better health care benefits and an increased minimum wage. He decentralized much of French governmental bureaucracy by increasing the authority of regional government administrations. Some of these new projects and laws met with considerable opposition by various groups of citizens. Decisions, such as the laying off of workers in the antiquated steel mills of northeastern France, caused unions to express their discontent.

President Mitterrand's answer to the many problems of France was the quest for a new society, one more oriented toward high technology and a more competitive stance in international trade. De Gaulle had urged his countrymen to cease their dependence on the United States and to shape their own destiny. Twenty five years later, France in the 1990s enjoys the world's second largest nuclear power system; the world's fastest passenger trains; and, in cooperation with other European states, a privately funded space program. France is also the world's fifth industrial power and the world's fourth leading exporter, evidence of its technological competitiveness and high-level research.

The Deux Magots,
on the Left Bank,
is one of the busiest
and most colorful
cafés in Paris.

French Culture

Florence Steiner, Ph.D.

A look at the map of Europe shows us that France has both natural and man-made boundaries. To the south, France is somewhat protected by the Pyrenees Mountains. It was actually the Pyrenees, a mountain range difficult to cross, that guaranteed a measure of independence for the French language, for had travelers been able to go readily from one part of the Roman Empire to the next, their linguistic differences would probably not have developed. It is less difficult to go into Italy, if one goes by the southern route. But traveling by northern routes, one must cross the Alps, a formidable natural boundary.

While natural boundaries are an advantage in time of war, they can impede trade in time of peace. The absence of such boundaries is an asset when one wishes to transport goods from one country to the next. An excellent railway systems links France to the rest of Europe. Within a few hours one can cross France and enter Spain, Italy, Switzerland, Germany, Belgium, England, Holland, or the Scandinavian countries.

It is a rewarding experience to rent a car in Paris and drive into southern France. The French are rapidly building toll roads and superhighways, called *autoroutes*. These are equal to the best American highways. At one moment the traveler is in the Parisian environment; less than two hours later he is watching the cathedral of Chartres rise from the plains. Should he direct himself westward, he will be at the historic Mont-St.-Michel, connected to the mainland only by a half-mile-long causeway during high tides. The abbey atop the mount is well worth visiting, and the one-street village that winds up its slope is famous for its omelets.

The traveler who directs himself southward from Paris enters the Loire Valley and the famous château country. He is struck by the sudden changes of scenery. From the plains he comes into mountainous territory with cascades and waterfalls, then to natural grottoes. Each province of France has its peculiar charm and gastronomic specialties, for cooking is one of the great interests of Frenchmen. Each province has made its special contribution to the national cuisine which has made French cooking famous throughout the world. Many regions produce their own kind of liqueur.

French Personality

Such a varied country can only produce people who are different: the fishermen of Brittany, the factory workers of Paris, the mountain dwellers of the Alps, the skilled technicians of Lille, the farmers of Normandy—the artist and the architect anywhere. One also notes with the change in land a change in temperament and people. The French are a people of contradictions: volatile, dramatic, and sensitive but also practical, stable, and traditional.

What brought about the French personality? Who *are* the French? Julius Caesar led his Roman legions into Gaul, where he found a people of Celtic descent whose priests were called druids. To these druids were confided the secrets, heritage, and educational precepts of the people. Caesar's army, in contrast, was composed of well-organized, practical men, of soldiers who spoke Latin. They were from Italy, which had not yet seen much of the northern, blond, barbarian invaders, an Italy of dark Mediterranean types. The Celtic peoples dwelling in Gaul were for the most part blond and light of complexion. So early France had a mixture of the Mediterranean or Latin type and the blond or Celtic type.

Although French women are in general short, attractive, and more brunette than blond, it is much more difficult to type the French as a whole than it is to type either the Spanish or the Italians. In our stereotyped picture of the Frenchman, we see him as a bon vivant, living his life gaily, drinking his wine, cutting off a hunk of bread, enjoying the company of the oposite sex, and being interested in paintings and art and music. But in reality our stereotype has many defects. Frenchmen—or some of them—may have certain of these attributes, but essentially French life revolves around the family. In France more than in the United States, we find many small family businesses, restaurants, and cafés in which husband and wife work side by side to secure the income of the family. Although divorce is increasing in France, as in the rest of the world, the Frenchman does not accept this solution to family problems lightly.

The French Family

The French mother is a power in the home. Contrary to opinion in this country, the French husband usually hands over the income to his wife, who administers it wisely and firmly. Children are under the close authority of their parents and the parents exercise their prerogatives freely. Today, more and more women in France work outside the home, particularly when there are no small children to care for.

A Frenchman is not as quick as his American counterpart to take a business associate home to dinner because this is an intrusion on family life, and the life of the family is most important to him. Nevertheless, in large cities one sees the advent of the business-cocktail party, and luncheon or dinner meetings in imitation of American business procedures.

French family life, contrary to some opinions, is very intimate. While French fathers play a dominant male role, it is the mother who in reality manages the house. French mothers are interested in seeing that their children develop well physically, and to this end they try to give them plenty of exercise and see that they have a balanced diet. French families go to great expense to send their youngsters on vacations either in the mountains or at the seaside. The primary reason for this is to ensure good health.

Another reason for this practice is that the French school day is so long that youngsters often do not have much time in which to play. Schools in France, like factories and shops, close between noon and two o'clock. This means that the school day is much longer than it is in the United States. Classes frequently end after five o'clock.

On Thursday afternoon there is no school, and children are taken to visit the museums of France to learn the history of their native villages or neighboring towns, to walk where famous people once promenaded, to see the ruins of a castle or a stained-glass window in an old cathedral, to see where battles were won or lost. France is a country whose history dates back to ancient times. The French have a long heritage of which to be proud, and the French family as a unit maintains this culture and transmits it from one generation to the next.

French children are very respectful to their parents for the most part. They are not likely to rebel against the dictums of father or mother, although they may experience the same inner rebellion that American youngsters experience. The family also shares many outings, such as picnics, dinners with relatives, sports events, afternoon walks, evening drives, and of course the inevitable vacation.

The French family vacation is the high point of the year. It is usually taken sometime during the month of August or perhaps September. The children, as mentioned earlier, often have been with the mother at the seashore or in the mountains. The father, having a month or more off from his job, may spend a few weeks camping or traveling with the family. French families do not feel obliged to spend the kind of money on vacations that American families do. They are perfectly happy to camp for two weeks by the side of a stream or to live in large groups, sometimes called colonies, near a seashore resort. Indeed, if a French mother cannot accompany her child or does not care to, she may send the child to a *colonie de vacances*. One will often see a hundred children walking to the seashore from a park or school where such a camp is located. The youngsters seem to enjoy these experiences very much, although this life may seem quite primitive to a tourist. Once the father joins the family for a vacation, the family operates as a unit and goes most places together. Baby-sitters, however, are also found in France nowadays.

The Riviera is a land unto itself, something the French know and may "warn" tourists about. In the months of July and August, the crowds at the Riviera are at their peak, and of course this is the time that Americans tend to frequent it. Food is at times expensive and hard to come by; hotel space is impossible, but this is because the French value the sea and the mountains as vacation spots for their children.

While Americans pay $150 to $200 a day for seaside rooms, along, say the Promenade des Anglais in Nice, a French mother and her child will be staying at a modest hotel a block or two from the beach and paying minimum prices, having made her reservations a year in advance. She may eat her breakfast at the hotel, or perhaps at a bar-café down the street. She will spend her mornings at the beach and she may enjoy a picnic lunch on her balcony, if she is fortunate enough to have one. This picnic lunch will consist of some freshly cooked roast pork (bought at the local grocery), a fresh tomato, a bit of French bread and cheese, and some fruit. For the child there will be fruit juice or mineral water, and the parent will have a glass of the local red wine. In the evening mother and child, having shopped around and read the menus posted outside, will go to a small restaurant where the proprietor will know them, give them a good table, and see that they are properly served. Knowing that the family will be there perhaps for a month or two, the proprietor will not charge exorbitant prices, for he knows that this will cause him to lose steady business and that he cannot always count on the tourist trade.

French Landscapes

If one remembers that France is roughly comparable in area to the state of Texas, he knows that this is not a small country, but neither is it a large one. France has an excellent system of railroads, the center of which is Paris. From Nice on the Riviera, one can take the *train bleu* and be in Paris approximately eight hours later. From Paris, in less time, one can be in Bordeaux on the Atlantic coast. From Paris one also has easy access to Switzerland, Germany, Belgium, Holland, and Denmark. If he enters France by ship and lands at Le Havre, he will find the drive to Paris an interesting one. Winding his way along the Seine, he sees barges transporting goods to the capital. He may stop at Rouen and see the marketplace and the plaque marking the spot where Joan of Arc was burned.

Or he may pass through the section called "the Stomach of Paris," Normandy, which produces a large amount of the agricultural products needed to feed the nation. Here prize cattle are raised, the butter is superb, apple orchards are everywhere and cider is the drink of the day—but cider with a bit of spark. Pancakes *(crêpes)* are also popular in this area.

Going southward along the coast from Normandy, one comes to the picturesque province of Brittany, the land of the ancient Celts, where we see ladies with high lace hats called *coiffes*. As we look at the ancient stone monuments, called menhirs, we may forcefully realize that here is a civilization different from that of the rest of France. This is fishing country, of boats that go out on the ocean and seem to repeat Victor Hugo's question: "Oh, how many sailors, how many husbands, how many sons, how many fathers have been lost?" Stalls of shimmering seafood and the religious processions of the maritime communities denote the influence of the sea on the lives of the people.

In the Pyrenees, farther south, it seems as if the ghost of Roland, one of the peers of Charlemagne, still persists. As the tourist approaches the Spanish border, the French language changes and we notice that it becomes less intelligible. This is not only due to the influence of Spanish but to a people who live in these mountains between Spain and France, the Basques. We don't really know where they came from, or whether they are an Indo-European people. Their language has remained a mystery to linguists but has been preserved to our day. They are a unique people, with their own customs and their own cuisine. Here in this land of waterfalls is the famous Cirque of Gavarnie, one of the great sights of France, a rounded glacial area coated entirely with ice and inaccessible except by horse or on foot.

East of Pau we come to the famous shrine of Lourdes. Each traveler has a mental picture of Lourdes but no picture is complete until he has been here. He senses an artificiality in the bouquets of flowers, the crucifixes, and the processions. But when he enters the city, he suddenly sees the sick, the lame, the blind, the crippled, not only from France but from countries all over the world. Now he sees the processions in a different light, and the prayers and the kneeling people, and suddenly he is in the middle of an experience that is difficult to recount. He visits the grotto, hears the stories, and leaves, but a part of him will never understand what he has just experienced.

If this variety of landscapes produces an equal variety of people, France has the stabilizing effect of a long history, and the record of that history is its monuments. Any visitor can recognize that the French are more than proud of their history and that their monuments at times are close to being sacred. French families will spend a Sunday or a Thursday afternoon at an art museum, at a cathedral, at a cemetery, or maybe at the home of a famous artist or author. French children see French monuments not once or twice but many, many times during their lifetime, and they can recite from memory the facts associated with these monuments.

Shopping

One of the favorite pastimes of French housewives is shopping for the day's food. One sees mothers on the streets any time from eight o'clock in the morning, occupied with their daily errands. The French do not usually provide bags for the various groceries, so the ladies carry a little net sack called a *filet*. The lady may enter the butcher shop first and select her meat for the day. The butcher wraps it in a very lightweight piece of paper and she puts it on the bottom of her *filet*. She probably is carrying several empty bottles to the market, which she will return to the grocer, and she will perhaps select a bottle of mineral water, a bottle of fruit juice, and, on occasion, a bottle of wine. She will proceed up the street, sometimes finding the vegetables set out for her inspection on the sidewalk, and she will select the vegetables and fruit that she needs. She will not let the store owner give her just any old apple or orange but will select each one with care and determination. As each of these items is paid for, into the *filet* it goes.

The lady may stop at a *crémerie* to select her butter and her milk. Not any butter will do, however; she may prefer a butter from Normandy. And while she is here she may also look for her favorite cheese. French cheeses are known by the regions from which they come. We speak, for example, of Camembert, which is a cheese that comes from the region of Camembert. Lastly the lady will enter the bakery, where she will see bread in all sizes and shapes: long thin loaves and rounded loaves. Probably she will select a *baguette.* This bread will be wrapped in a cloth and sliced throughout the day. Some of it may remain until the next morning, when it will be toasted for the family breakfast.

Like many French traditions, leisurely shopping in specialty shops is becoming less common today in France, particularly in large urban areas. As more and more French women begin to work outside the home, supermarkets with one-stop shopping are replacing many of the traditional specialty shops.

French Food

In rural France the main meal is always served at noon, and whenever possible members of the family come home for the noonday meal. If properly done, this meal is no simple affair, and for this reason French shops usually close between the hours of noon and 2:00 p.m. so that the owners may enjoy a lunch at leisure and a short nap afterwards.

What do the French eat for lunch? Usually an appetizer, or as the French say *pour commencer* (to begin with). This may be a series of *hors d'oeuvre,* perhaps grated carrots, grated celery root, some raw cucumbers sliced. Sometimes it will be tomato salad, which in France is just that, sliced tomatoes—perhaps sprinkled with parsley, oil, and vinegar. Sometimes the first course is seafood. (On the Riviera one may have mussels cooked in wine sauce. For tourists, one favorite is a French omelet.) The second course is usually a meat course. This may vary from a small steak served with very crisp french-fried potatoes, and a veal cutlet cooked in cream and garnished with mushrooms, to chicken delicately roasted and perhaps served with potatoes. This is considered the main course (the word for "course" is *plat.*) When you see *plat du jour* on a menu, this means that items are the day's specialty, and frequently the price is attractive. The French finish their normal noonday meal with either cheese or dessert, sometimes both. The cheese may vary from goat cheese to Gruyère, and a real favorite is yogurt. During the summer they prefer fresh fruit; ice cream and pastries are frequently available.

If the meal is served at home and guests are invited, five or six courses may be served. These can include the *hors-d'oeuvre,* then a fish, then a meat, then a salad or vegetable, then cheese, then dessert or fruit, and finally a liqueur with coffee. This is why, if a French housewife is having guests for luncheon, she may spend most of the morning shopping and cooking so that she can present a meal of which she will be proud.

When the family can assemble at noon and have the main meal together, the evening meal is relatively light. It would begin with *potage,* a thick soup which is made by cooking vegetables such as carrots, onions, and potatoes and putting them through a sieve. Tapioca is usually added to the vegetable juice to thicken it, then seasonings are added, and the strained vegetables are now put in. Following the soup course, one might have some of the noonday meat served cold. This would be followed by a vegetable and a salad. If cheese were served at noon, dessert would be served in the evening, or vice versa. For the French housewife, the evening meal is easier if her family is home. However, with the advent of factories and with many people working in the city, the French housewife, like her American counterpart, now prepares her major meal in the evening.

The Workday

French office workers and others still enjoy the leisurely two-hour lunch, and restaurants do not expect to serve one group of customers, have them leave, and quickly serve another group—as American restaurants do. Indeed, the usual clientele will come and stay, and this is what French restaurant owners expect.

However, the habits of the American businessmen have been copied, and many Frenchmen now take a very light and quick lunch so that they may conduct their business more effectively during the afternoon. Because of this long lunch hour, French offices and shops tend to stay open later than those in the United States. As stated, one will frequently find shops open until seven in the evening.

In order to survive the long business day, the Frenchman along about four or five o'clock will take what is commonly called the *apéritif.* This may be only a soft drink, such as a Coca-Cola or an Orange Crush or a glass of lemon juice served with sugar and a pitcher of water. He may, however, request a small cup of concentrated coffee, but more than likely he will have a glass of wine or a sweet drink. He usually goes to his favorite café and has this drink in a leisurely fashion, perhaps talking to some friends, perhaps watching the girls stroll by. He may buy a paper and read it if no one is in the café whom he knows. He does not have to worry about being hurried since no good French waiter would consider asking a person to move on if he had not finished his drink.

The café is a popular place all during the day. In the early morning, excellent coffee and rolls (called *croissants*) are served in the small bar-cafés of the city. Some cafés also serve meals, sandwiches, or snacks.

French Educational System

The French educational system has been undergoing major reforms since France has of late been suffering from a scarcity of technicians, doctors, and the like. For many years the system devoted itself primarily to producing an educational elite, and the quality of the French system can scarcely be questioned. Nevertheless, since 1959 there have been some major changes. More young people are continuing their education, and education is compulsory until age sixteen.

The French system is composed of kindergarten, which is optional, and a five-year elementary program followed by a four-year cycle of intermediate studies called secondary education. At the end of this time the student may elect a terminal course or a two-year course that leads to a diploma, or *brevet,* that will allow him to enter skilled occupations, public service, railway work, etc. He may elect the longer term of three years, and at the end of this time present himself as a candidate for the *baccalauréat*. The famous *bac* is his admission ticket to the university, but to achieve it he must compete in a national exam. About the earliest he can obtain the *bac* is around age eighteen. Then, as in the United States, he must decide which section of the university he will enter. As a matter of fact, he will have taken his *bac* in one of five areas: (1) literature, languages, and philosophy; (2) social sciences; (3) math and physics; (4) experimental sciences and math; (5) math and technical sciences.

The French universities are true institutions of higher learning. They do not, for example, offer many beginning language courses except in the exotic languages. (One is expected to have a command of a foreign language before entering the university.) Attendance at class is not mandatory but the exams are all important. Sometimes they are in the form of *concours,* competitive exams that only a certain number (perhaps only ten) can pass, no matter how many strong candidates present themselves. Of course, one can always try again at the next *coucours* if he is unsuccessful.

There are several degrees one might get at the university level. The first is a diploma called the *Diplôme Universitaire d'Etudes Littéraires,* or one may try for the *licence,* which corresponds roughly to our master's degree. Or one may get the new degree, the *maîtrise,* which demands an additional year. If one goes on to the *agrégation,* he is entitled to teach at the higher levels of the lycée. Finally, after about ten years of research, he may present himself for the *doctorat,* for which he must write a thesis and defend it before a jury or committee.

The "great schools" *(Grandes Ecoles)* are institutions that prepare candidates for specialized work, for example, the School of Mines, the School of Electricity, etc. One is admitted via the *concours* or competitive examination, and since there are so few of these schools for the number of candidates, admission is highly selective. Indeed, many French technicians are trained outside of France. Two great schools in Paris are the University of Paris, of which the Sorbonne is a part, and the College of France, which is much more liberal. All a professor has to do in the latter is give a certain number of lectures, which are open to the public. This school was founded by Francis I during the Renaissance. Its mission was to give a more liberal education than the Sorbonne, which was primarily occupied in preparing priests and monks.

Today the trend in France is toward educating a greater segment of the population. As more people are enrolled in the educational institutions, as the poor as well as the wealthy have a chance to be educated, France is facing many of the same problems that arise in the United States. Students in France have always made their presence felt. They have fought at barricades, they have been members of the underground, and it is not surprising to find that they have also engaged in student riots. Though in most instances they lack the campuses, fraternities and sororities, and the sports that are found on American campuses, French students have always been interested in causes and politics.

French students have always been given a measure of privileged treatment by the government. Even foreign students traveling in France can secure coupons that give them reduced railway fares, the right to eat in certain student restaurants that are much less expensive than others, and lodging at minimum prices. The French student does not expect to work while he is studying, and he frequently has little or no spending money. He will study in public parks or gardens or the local café. He socializes, but in a different way than his American counterpart. In recent years large numbers of American university students have found French campuses an excellent place to learn not only the language but the art, history, and culture of a people.

Because of the highly competitive nature of French education and the importance of passing such exams as those for the *bac* or the *concours,* French parents and youngsters place much importance on education from the very start.

The French Academy

Like all august bodies, the French Academy and its members have received their share of ribbing throughout the centuries. Sometimes called "the Immortals" since the members occupy their places until their death, sometimes called "the Great Forty," since membership is limited to forty members, the academy is considered one of France's greatest institutions. Originally founded by Richelieu in 1634, the academy was charged with the production of a dictionary. The academy today, composed of the literary elite, is charged with preserving the integrity and purity of the French language. For over three centuries the honor of membership was reserved for French men and no foreigners were eligible. In 1980, however, the academy elected Marguerite Yourcenar, the first woman ever honored with membership. Yourcenar, Belgian-born, had moved to the United States in 1950 and became a naturalized U.S. citizen.

Election to membership in the academy depends partly upon the death of one of the academicians. Various candidates are proposed, many of whom are chosen from the outstanding writers of the day. When the vote is finally taken, the winner is received in a ceremony in which he presents a eulogy of his predecessor, and another member of the academy presents a eulogy of the new member. A special outfit is worn by the academy members on state occasions. Because this uniform is green, a particularly ambitious candidate is said to suffer from *fièvre verte* (''green fever''). The academy published the ninth edition of its dictionary in 1986, updating the eighth edition of 1935. There is usually a fifty-year gap between editions.The *Grammaire* of the academy appeared in 1932 in very simple form, and since that time there has been no succeeding edition.

Summary

What is the Frenchman's philosophy? That is difficult to say, just as it would be difficult to summarize the philosophy of an American. One can say, however, that the Frenchman works in order to have enough money to enjoy life; money for him is a means to an end. He knows that life is short and he values each day for what it is. He is willing to take time to enjoy life—to visit with a friend at a café, to sit in a park and enjoy the beauty around him, to discuss politics with a friend or relative.

His background and heritage are a part of him, not something to be put aside and considered only one or two days a year. Paris is his city; its monuments belong to him, and he expects the government to maintain them in good condition.

He is interested in ideas—in philosophy and politics. He has a favorite newspaper, which he reads avidly, and he has his own solutions to national problems.

The French love for freedom is beautifully portrayed in this famous painting, *La Liberté guidant le peuple,* by Eugène Delacroix.

French Art History

L. Herse

Prehistoric French art, or art that appeared in what today is France, began 10,000, 15,000, or perhaps even 20,000 years ago (scholars are not certain) in the caves of southwestern France, in a region called Dordogne. It was in this area, in fact, that paleolithic art was born, created by the crude hands of man, the Old Stone Age inhabitants, living in shelters or excavations inside mountains or caverns under the surface of the earth.

Since its discovery, the caveman's art has interested artists and continues to arouse the interest of artists and scholars the world over. They have come to Dordogne to admire and study the beautiful rock carvings and designs in bold black and red colors on the cave walls and ceilings.

The best sites of prehistoric art in southwest France are the caves at Lascaux (Dordogne), the la Magdeleine cave at Penne, and the Font-de-Gaume caves (also in the Dordogne region), where murals and frescoes of bison, deer, horses, cattle, and even the human figure (believed to be a symbolic image) represent the best "underground" art gallery ever to be discovered.

The Roman Period

Historic French art originated in the years just prior to the birth of Christ, during the celebrated era of the Roman Empire. After 50 B.C., the time of the conquest of Gaul (present-day France) by the mighty Roman army led by Julius Caesar, France was under the influence of the Greco-Roman culture. Its artistic trends, similar to the trends adopted in its countries of origin—Italy and the other parts of the empire—were soon to expand throughout every region of the new colony. The Roman style manifested itself primarily in grandiose architectural projects, which became the most admired creations of this period.

Living in an era of fast expansionism and even faster population growth, Roman architects and builders looked to the practical side of life rather than to pure art and theoretical expressions. Pressed by the need for increased numbers of living quarters to accommodate the many thousands of new citizens of Rome, their creative power delivered several practical innovations in the field of civil engineering. Architecture became a full-scale operation after the discovery of cement or concrete as the most durable and dependable building material.

With the introduction of cement, used in place of the Greek freestone, Roman architects and engineers developed a massive, functional style of arches, columns, and vaults (arched roofs and ceilings), which proved very practical in the construction of all urban buildings.

This rugged type of architecture dominated the Roman Empire—from Rome, its capital, to the colonial countrysides. In France, one of the best examples of Roman construction is the perfectly preserved aqueduct at Nîmes, in southern France, built in the early first century A.D. The aqueduct of Pont du Gard, as it is called, is a colonial pipeline erected more than 150 feet above the ground and composed of massive arches, one on top of the other, designed to bring fresh water to the rural population.

Besides architectural masterpieces such as the aqueducts, fine examples of statuary, monuments, and a variety of sculptures—all of them typical of the French-Roman era—are preserved in museums of antiquities and in art galleries throughout France. The Louvre, in Paris, houses a valuable collection of fragments and sculptured objects dating from several centuries before the birth of Christ.

As western Europe began to approach that period in history known as the Middle Ages, the glory of Rome fading slowly away, a new civilization was setting the stage for the next several centuries.

During the first 300 years, while the difficult road to Christianity was being prepared by the early Christian refugees and martyrs, the history of art continued to be written throughout despite long years of harsh opposition and persecutions. On the walls of catacombs the faithful, in symbolic images and sacred scenes, wrote the history of creation and kept art alive. From the art of the early Christian era, also known as the art of the catacombs, sprang the inspirations which gave rise to the art of the Middle Ages.

After Emperor Constantine (during the course of the fourth century) embraced Christianity and accepted it as the official religion of the Roman communities, the previously hidden art of the catacombs was brought out into the open. This historic move initiated a series of great movements in sacred art and the traditional notion of the church as an architectural masterpiece of beauty and value. The church, acting as custodian of Middle Ages' art treasures, preserved some of the most ambitious creations ever conceived and executed by humans.

Under Constantine, Byzantium replaced Rome as the new capital of the Roman Empire. Thus for the next several centuries, Europe became the recipient of a largely foreign culture, that of Constantinople (present-day Istanbul). Oriental motifs and themes, until then unknown among the Mediterranean civilizations and the cultures north of the Alps, made their first appearance in western Europe.

The influence of Byzantium on a Europe thoroughly absorbed by the religious sentiment that prevailed throughout the area after the fourth century stimulated one of the most creative art periods in the history of the world. Led by Constantinople's school of thought, architecture and sculpture flourished for several centuries.

French-Romanesque Art

After the sixth and seventh centuries, however, a new element made deep inroads and greatly influenced the Byzantine concepts and styles of the Middle Age church. The impact upon western Europe of successive invasions by Germanic tribes from north of the Alps was a succession of various cultures which, in turn, became embedded in the traditions of the Christian church.

The invasion of France by a Germanic people called the Franks (from whom France derived its post-Roman name), left indelible traces in the history of that country, traces which became rooted in the artistic expressions of a style known today as Romanesque. *Romanesque,* meaning "partly Roman," because of its adoption of classical themes, was the unique architectural style of most French church structures erected during and after the reign of Charlemagne—from the ninth to the twelfth century.

Romanesque architecture, also called "the art of the monks," was employed by monastic orders such as the Cistercians and Carthusians, who presided over the construction of abbeys, churches, and monasteries, all of them adorned with a profusion of sculptured portraits, carvings, and stained-glass artwork.

French Romanesque art reached its zenith in the eleventh century with the construction of immense buildings that featured rugged vaults, arches, and columns patterned after the Italian basilicas, the Roman tribunals and communal meeting places of the past.

The most perfect examples of French Romanesque art (and perhaps the best in Europe) are the Church of St. Sernin at Toulouse (southern France), the Cathedral of Autun (Burgundy), the Church of St. Savin-sur-Gartempe (in western France), and in the historic region of Normandy (northern France), where a blend of Romanesque and Anglo-Norman styles inspired the beautiful abbey of St. Etienne (founded in Caen by William the Conqueror during the eleventh century).

In painting, the best contributions originated inside the church itself, where the religious communities—in addition to large wall pictures and frescoes—introduced a new art form known as manuscript illumination or the adornment of sacred writings. The most numerous examples of this unique art are found in northern France, an important center of monastic life and activities.

Gothic Art

The blend of many influences—Greco-Roman, Byzantine, and Romanesque—gave birth in the twelfth through the fourteenth century to the most important European art style since that of classical Greece: the Gothic style.

The most valuable aspect of French Gothic art lies in the fact that it did not remain confined to one illustrious era in the history of a country or region, but hurdled local boundaries to become universally acclaimed and popular for many centuries. A symbol of perfection, French Gothic architecture was highly admired and imitated abroad in the planning of such ambitious buildings and town halls as the Doges' Palace in Venice and the Palazzo Vecchio in Florence.

It was, however, in the field of church structure that Gothic art made its most impressive contribution. Also known as the era of the cathedrals, the Gothic age gave the world some of its most sumptuous churches. In the cathedrals, the most outstanding innovations consisted of enormous stained-glass windows, high vaults, portals (or doorways), and hundreds of biblical-scene carvings and sculptures as general ornamentation of the facades.

France and England became known as the cradle of Gothic art, and it is in these two countries that the most acclaimed Gothic churches are located. The golden age of this art reached its zenith during the second half of the twelfth century, a period known also as the high Gothic Age.

In France, the high Gothic years were responsible for the construction of such architectural masterpieces as the abbey-church of St. Denis in Paris, Chartres Cathedral (featuring a design composed of about 10,000 sculptured figures), Amiens Cathedral, the cathedral of Reims (built in the thirteenth century), and the most spectacular of all Gothic achievements, the cathedral of Notre-Dame in Paris (begun in 1163).

Perhaps one of the most interesting innovations of the church during the high Gothic era was the floor plan designed in the shape of a cross, the basic plan for most of the cathedrals built during and after this period. Symbolic of the crucifixion, most of the cathedrals were dedicated to the memory of the Virgin Mary.

With the end of the thirteenth century, the highest peak of Gothic architecture was reached and a new phase set in: a closing phase known as flamboyant or late Gothic. The late Gothic years were characterized by an interest in intricate designs and ornaments, generally overlying the basic skeletons of the structures. Elaborate examples of flamboyant Gothic appeared throughout France in the erection of castles, town halls, and churches like Saint-Maclou in Rouen. The Louvre in Paris, first built in the thirteenth century in the austerity of the Gothic tradition, was later "remodeled" (during the reign of Charles V in the fourteenth century), as a flamboyant-type residence for royalty.

Besides the continuation of manuscript adornment initiated by Romanesque artists, the most outstanding pictorial contributions are preserved inside the churches and cathedrals, where stained-glass work reached a stage of perfection in the skillful hands of Gothic masters. With the creation of immense translucent windows—some of them as tall as 14 feet and completely covered with jigsaw patterns of fragmented figures—the artists succeeded in providing the faithful with a sense of "closeness to the high heavens."

Some illustrations and geometrical designs of cathedral windows are contained in a sketchbook by a thirteenth-century architect, Villard de Honnecourt. The sketchbook is preserved in the Bibliothèque Nationale in Paris.

The Renaissance

The Renaissance did not express itself north of the Alps the same way it did in Italy. While Florence and Rome, the centers of Renaissance art, drew most of their inspiration from antiquity, with classical Greece as the focal point of their new interest, northern Europe developed rather slowly along the well-established Gothic tradition rooted in the customs and taste of the French and English communities.

During the early part of the fifteenth century, France still derived most of its influence from Germany and Flanders (part of present-day Belgium). The foremost French exponent of the early Renaissance years (sometimes called the late Gothic years) was Jean Fouquet, a painter whose work in gold, copper, and enamel (a self-portrait) is at the Louvre in Paris.

Significant signs of Italian Renaissance influence did not begin to appear until the end of the fifteenth century, in paintings (such as *The Avignon Picta,* executed in southern France by an unknown master) and in an assortment of sculptures, such as the statues, monuments, and portraits used in the ornamentation of pulpits, tombs, and private residences rather than in grandiose architectural projects.

As the Italian Renaissance began to approach its golden era during the sixteenth century, highlighted by the works of Michelangelo, Raphael, and Leonardo da Vinci, France came more and more under the influence of the classic style dear to the Florentine school.

In the field of sculpture, Jean de Boulogne (known in Italy as Giovanni Bologna) distinguished himself while studying under the guidance of Italian masters. Among his works, a marble statue called *The Rape of the Sabine Women* still has a place of honor near the Palazzo Vecchio in Florence.

The peak of the French Renaissance was reached during the sixteenth century under the reign of King Francis I, an art connoisseur who liked to surround himself and the people of his court with the leading painters of the day. During his reign the famous château of Fontainebleau, near Paris, was built. The château, a summer residence for kings, was constructed and decorated in the finest Italian Renaissance tradition by sculptor Benvenuto Cellini and interior decorator Primaticcio.

Under Francis I, the visual arts flourished and grew. Architecture, in particular, reached a standard of utmost prestige after the construction of part of the Louvre's "square court," designed by Pierre Lescot, an eminent architect. The Louvre's addition is one of the most complete examples of French Renaissance art in its classical phase.

In sculpture, the leading names of the sixteenth century were Jean Goujon, the creator of the beautiful Fontaine des Innocents in Paris, and Germain Pilon, who sculptured the monumental tomb of King Henry II (featuring bronze statues and marble reliefs) inside the Church of St. Denis in Paris.

The Baroque Period

The era of French baroque art evolved along the trends created by the Italian baroque schools. It was in Italy, in fact, that the reaction to Renaissance classicism originated, around the beginning of the seventeenth century.

The baroque interpretation was born of a need to explore new forms and avenues leading to a somewhat different art concept after long years of classic "perfectionism." Experimenting with various ideas and themes, Italian artists discovered a new style: a highly decorative form of ornamentation which showed a flare for "the unconventional and the elaborate." This style was called baroque, from *barroco,* an unusual pearl of irregular shape.

While the baroque era in Italy witnessed the partial eclipse of centuries of leadership by that country in the field of the visual arts, baroque art is remembered in France as opening a glorious period during which Paris became the new capital of the art world. The upsurge of the baroque style coincided with a historic period of great importance during which France, under the leadership of one of its most influential monarchs, Louis XIV, became the most powerful nation in the western world and the unsurpassed setter and tutor of taste and style.

Baroque art, which fitted the atmosphere of opulence and grandeur in the French court, soon became known as the "royal style," or the "style of Louis XIV," an expression which is still popular in modern circles. Some scholars like to compare the splendor of the French baroque era to the Italian high Renaissance of a century earlier.

Among the most prominent painters of this period we must single out Georges de la Tour (*Joseph the Carpenter* [in the Louvre]), Louis le Nain (*Peasant Family* [the Louvre]), and Nicolas Poussin, who was internationally acclaimed for his mythological subjects and landscapes (*The Burial of Phocion* [the Louvre]).

Claude Lorrain later made notable contributions as a proficient landscapist, versatile in the handling of pastoral scenes, such as *The View of the Campagna* (in the British Museum, London).

In architecture the foremost contributions were made by François Mansart, the designer of famous châteaus, such as the Château de Maisons near Paris. Louis le Vau, Charles Lebrun, and Claude Perrault, three outstanding designers and architects, were credited with two of the most important accomplishments of this era. The first was the completion of the Louvre, a marvelous example of classical architecture, which was converted during the eighteenth century into a museum containing such art treasures as Leonardo da Vinci's *Mona Lisa,* marble statues by

Michelangelo, and many other masterpieces. The second was the construction of the Palace of Versailles, the luxurious residence of Louis XIV outside Paris, which contained a magnificent collection of valuable paintings, lavish royal apartments, and the famous Hall of Mirrors *(Galerie des Glaces),* renowned the world over for its elegance and ornate decor. The chief interior decorator of the age, under whose watchful eye the Palace of Versailles was completed, was the artist Charles Lebrun. The designer responsible for its exterior and for the formal gardens, terraces, and statuary adorning the palace's vast park was Le Notre. A skillful architect, Jules Hardouin-Mansart, is known for the *Eglise des Invalides,* built in Paris at the end of the seventeenth century.

An important event which had an enduring effect on the history of the visual arts in France took place during the reign of Louis XIV. It was caused, or rather promoted, by a group of highly trained and ambitious artists close to the royal circle who became interested in a more refined and sophisticated type of training, different from the popular apprenticeship programs in vogue since Renaissance times.

With the official approval of Louis XIV in 1648, the king's artists founded the Royal Academy of Painting and Sculpture in Paris, a formal institution which provided a course of studies complete with practical and theoretical training according to an exclusive curriculum prepared by the *académiciens* themselves. The Royal Academy—and its high standards—thus laid the foundations for all modern art schools and academies throughout the world.

At the beginning of the eighteenth century, however, after the death of Louis XIV, a change in the attitude of the French people and institutions began to manifest itself in an atmosphere of more relaxed expression, somewhat released from the imposed taste of the king and his royal entourage. This feeling of independence was coined by late seventeenth-century artists they called rococo style, a highly individualistic interpretation of baroque art adapted to more extravagant and exuberant tastes. Rococo painting became known as *l'art du boudoir,* for it developed mainly inside the palatial residences of the aristocracy, where affluence and frivolity permitted excesses in style and taste. Of all the best-known painters of this era of decadence, Antoine Watteau headed the list. His best works, such as *A Pilgrimage to Cythera,* are part of the Louvre's art treasury.

Along with Watteau, Jean-Baptiste Simeon Chardin distinguished himself for his domestic scenes, such as his expressive *Back from the Market* (the Louvre), while François Boucher, a favorite of Louis XV, and Jean-

Honoré Fragonard made names for themselves as the most sought-after "boudoir" or court painters of the pre-revolution era. Fragonard's famous *Bathers* is also on view at the Louvre.

Neoclassicism and Romanticism

The rococo years represented the closing phase of royal France's "official" style and the onset of a revolutionary movement which matured during many turbulent years of political instability. After decades of regimented court styles and taste, a cry for freedom was raised by young painters anxious to discard the frivolity of "boudoir art" for a more serious and sensitive approach to art and its expressions. Nostalgia for the past and for the calm beauty of antiquity began to reappear, while a desire to explore the classical sources of Rome and Greece once more became an irresistible stimulus among the most serious students.

A longing for sincerity and the spontaneous appreciation of life and nature, feelings which until then had been hidden under a blanket of artificiality, inaugurated a period called the neoclassic and romantic.

Sentimentalism and a love for the simple life inspired some of the most beautiful landscapes ever painted on canvas. Rural scenes, peaceful sunsets, and idyllic panoramas became some of the landscapists' favorite subjects, while portrait artists dedicated themselves to the re-creation of the human scene in its simplest forms.

Among the leading representatives of the neoclassic era, special credit must be given to Jacques-Louis David, the father of the movement, and a revolutionary soldier, who expressed his deepest emotions in a masterpiece titled *The Death of Marat,* (on view at the Royal Museum of Fine Arts in Brussels). One of his landscapes, *The Luxembourg Gardens,* is exhibited at the Louvre.

Besides David, Auguste-Dominique Ingres, whose works are a part of the world's most famous collections, became known as one of the true giants of neoclassic art. His celebrated portrait, *Louis Bertin,* is exhibited in the Louvre, along with some of his other masterpieces.

A more violent attitude was expressed in the works of Theodore Géricault, as in *Mounted Officer of the Imperial Guard* (the Louvre). Eugene Delacroix, the giant among romantic painters and a rival of Ingres, gained fame for his dramatic subjects, such as *Liberty Leading the People* and *The Massacre of Chios,* both of which are in the Louvre. Honoré Daumier was a romanticist whose washerwomen are well-known the world over. His famous *Third-Class Carriage* is exhibited at the Metropolitan Museum of Art in New York.

In sculpture, the major contributions were made by Jean Antoine Houdon, known on this side of the Atlantic for his famous bust of George

Washington at the Metropolitan Museum of Art in New York. François Rude created *La Marseillaise,* a ''rhetorical''statue carved on the Arc de Triomphe in Paris. Antoine-Louis Barye became famous for his bronzes, such as *Jaguar Devouring a Hare* (the Louvre). Jean-Baptiste Carpeaux created the elegant statue called *The Dance,* executed on the façade of the Paris Opera.

In architecture, the classical style of Greece reappeared—along with reborn Gothic trends—in the construction of the Pantheon, a great monument by Jacques Germain Soufflot, and in the famous Paris Opera, designed by Charles Garnier in the mid-nineteenth century in a mixed style of baroque and romantic.

The Modern Period

When we speak of the modern age we are referring to a series of periods in art which stemmed from common ideological roots during the second half of the nineteenth century and a good portion of the twentieth century. By "modern age" we do not connote just the arts and talents of contemporary masters, living or deceased, but rather the various trends which have existed for at least one hundred years and more or less became assimilated into *one* school of thought.

In order to understand the substance of these thoughts, we must go back to approximately the middle of the nineteenth century, when photography (part of the industrial revolution) came of age and made its first appearance—or rather intrusion—in the artist's life.

With the advent of photography and its new way of making portraits and landscapes, the hand and eye of the artist—until then the only "camera" capable of reproducing reality—lost its place of honor. Fearing the keen competition of this modern rival, the artist began to look beyond the limits of reality for inspiration and subject matter. From this search for "an ideal," an entirely new attitude was born: that of art in its purest forms, unrestricted by academic standards or tradition, highly original and spontaneous.

France was to be the cradle of "freedom of expression," and it was here that the modern age was born. A series of movements developed which brought French art to one of its highest levels.

Realism and Impressionism

One of the first movements to detach itself completely from the traditions of the past became known as the school of the realists, who were—the school's founder Gustave Courbet frankly admitted—"the artists who refused to paint angels because they could not see any." This independence of spirit, indeed revolutionary for nineteenth-century France, caught on—as time was to witness during the coming years. For Courbet, realism was a lack of the kind of sentimentality associated with the romanticists and a rejection of the stylization that characterized the neoclassicists.

His principles and beliefs are best reflected in his celebrated *Mon Atelier* (My Studio), a canvas that is 20 feet long and covered with life-size figures taken from the real world: peasants, hunters, intellectuals, children, etc. This colorful painting, depicting the human scene of nineteenth-century France as it appeared to Courbet, is part of the Louvre's permanent collection.

Following in Courbet's footsteps, another advocate of absolute freedom of expression, Edouard Manet, emphasized geometric patterns and broken color schemes. He painted boldly and simply, presenting a concept of "free" composition which was a prelude to Picasso's cubism. His anticonventional pictures, such as *The Fifer* and *Luncheon on the Grass* (both at the Louvre), conveyed a message and techniques which were understood and followed by all subsequent modern-age movements.

Claude Monet opened the way to the most popular of nineteenth-century schools of thought in painting: impressionism. The word was coined by coincidence, when one of Monet's paintings (now a masterpiece) was first shown to the public, in 1874, at a private exhibition held in a prominent photographer's studio. The painting, titled *Sunrise: An Impression,* was publicly ridiculed by several art critics who denounced it as an unfinished piece of art done without taste by an untrained hand. Monet was consequently called an "impressionist."

Monet's works, mainly lively and sunlit landscapes, became part of the world's best art collections. His style was greatly admired by other famous impressionists, such as Renoir, Degas, Toulouse-Lautrec, Rousseau, Van Gogh, Seurat, Gauguin, Cézanne, and Bonnard—whose masterpieces represent the greatest contributions of nineteenth-century France to world art.

Auguste Renoir was known as a happy man and happy painter. His vitality and good humor is found throughout his work, mostly faces of chubby children, sunny outdoor scenes, noisy cafés and bars of the Latin Quarter and bohemian Paris, and female models aglow in arrays of color. One of his best paintings, *Le Moulin de la Galette* (at the Louvre), attained international acclaim—along with many other oil paintings, pastels, and chalk drawings collected by renowned museums throughout the world. Among his portraits in oil, *Gabrielle, A Woman Reading,* and *Gabrielle with a Rose* (all at the Louvre) deserve special recognition.

Edgard Degas' work, often done in pastels (dry crayons), reflects the style of other impressionists, as evidenced in his colorful studies of ballerinas, his still lifes, and female nudes. *The Tub, Prima Ballerina,* and

The Glass of Absinthe (all at the Louvre) are some of the best examples of his talents as a painter.

Henri de Toulouse-Lautrec, the son of a nobleman, was a cripple who preferred the atmosphere of bohemian life in Paris to the security of a comfortable future in his hometown in southern France. He shared his life in Paris with underworld characters, café entertainers, and a variety of desperados who lived in the slums.

His experiences were immortalized in beautiful oils and lithographs, which have been collected by various museums; the Albi Museum, in Lautrec's home town, probably contains the best selection of his work.

The originator of the modern poster, Toulouse-Lautrec gave the art world one of its most vivid collections of poster subjects: theater personalities, cancan dancers, café characters, etc. Of his posters, *At the Moulin Rouge* and *Troupe de Mlle Eglantine* (both at the Art Institute of Chicago) are considered among his best efforts.

Vincent Van Gogh was born in Holland but lived most of his professional life in Paris, where—as was the case with many of his artist friends—his talent thrived in the midst of a bohemian life and café atmosphere. His preoccupation with dazzling colors and sunlight is revealed in all his work, particularly in his famous *Sunflowers* (at the Metropolitan Museum of Art in New York).

Van Gogh is classified as a great Dutch master in Holland, where in his younger days he painted one of his rare non-impressionist canvases, *The Potato Eaters* (in the collection of V. W. van Gogh in Laren, Holland), which reflects the somber mood inspired by his early life as a preacher among Belgian coal miners.

Paul Gauguin, one of Van Gogh's friends, shared much of his colleague's fascination for vivid colors and contrast. His passion for the exotic produced a large collection of unique paintings executed in a primitive childlike style while he lived among the natives of Tahiti. His Tahitian pictures, exhibited in the renowned galleries of the world, have been a major contribution to modern art.

Paul Cézanne's main contribution to French art was his singular interpretation of objects and people as geometric patterns and lines. His fondness for the structure of things rather than for their finished details is best reflected in such outstanding works as *The Card Players* (in a private collection in New York) and *Fruit Bowl, Glass, and Apples* (a still life in the Lecampto Collection in Paris).

Henri Rousseau has been called the "innocent" among the French impressionists. His childlike talent, spontaneous and fanciful, developed highly decorative pictures and drawings which resemble illustrations in fairy-tale books. Among his best works, *The Dream* and *The Sleeping*

Beauty (both in the Museum of Modern Art in New York) are typical examples of his imaginative style.

Georges Seurat, best known for his patterned compositions resembling wallpaper or fabric designs, did not produce many paintings. His method, very intricate and technical, required a perfectionist's patience. Of his pictures, consisting of showers of tiny specks and dots, *A Sunday Afternoon at La Grande Jatte* (in the Art Institute of Chicago) is one of the best examples of his difficult style.

Pierre Bonnard was the last of the great impressionist painters. His *Breakfast Room* (at the Museum of Modern Art in New York) summarizes the impressionist idea of free composition and color contrast.

In sculpture, the mood of the times was best caught by Auguste Rodin, who became known for his powerfully constructed bronze and marble figures, such as *The Thinker* (Metropolitan Museum of Art, New York) and *The Kiss* (Rodin Museum, Paris). In the execution of his sculpture, Rodin followed the impressionists' technique of using simplified, geometric forms, a concept which became a fundamental of twentieth-century art.

The Twentieth Century

With the opening of the twentieth century, the post-impressionist era began to emerge with its own characteristics and distinctions. There were signs of independence and maturity. Individuality and difference in expression characterized its three main currents: expressionism, which stresses the artist's attitude toward himself and the world; abstract art, which is concerned largely with the formal structure of a work; and fantasy, which explores the spontaneous and irrational qualities of the imagination.

One of the most celebrated members of the first movement, Henri Matisse, is famous for his "primitive" paintings, such as *The Moroccans* (Museum of Modern Art, New York), the *Odalisk with Red Trousers* (National Museum of Modern Art, Paris) and the *Sideboard* (National Museum of Modern Art, Paris). Georges Rouault was another famous expressionist, whose *Head of Christ* (W. Chrysler Jr. Collection, New York) is a very liberal interpretation of subject matter.

The most famous member of the abstract movement was Pablo Picasso, a Spaniard by birth, who in the early 1900s originated the concept of cubism, or facet painting, which became very popular in the years that followed. Among his best creations are *The Three Musicians, Girl before a Mirror* (both at the Museum of Modern Art, New York), and *Guernica* (Casón del Buen Retiro, Madrid, Spain).

A friend and follower of Picasso, Georges Braque, created similar cubistic pictures (see *Man with a Guitar* in the Museum of Modern Art in New York).

The most respected member of the pure fantasy movement is Marc Chagall, a Russian-born painter who lived in Paris. One of his best-known pictures, *I and the Village* (Museum of Modern Art, New York), is a colorful "fairy tale" of lights and shadows.

In sculpture, the trends of abstract and cubist interpretations, mingled with expressionistic influences, found their best spokesmen in Constantin Brancusi, known for his *Kiss* (a monument for Montparnasse Cemetery in Paris), and Alberto Giacometti, who is also a follower of "constructivism," a form of sculpture which utilizes various scraps and materials, such as wood, metal, string, and wire. One of Giacometti's works, *The Palace at 4 A.M.,* is exhibited in the Museum of Modern Art in New York.

In architecture, the new look was introduced by a man known simply as Le Corbusier. Le Corbusier's stature during the course of this century rose high above his tall and unusual buildings. By modifying and rejuvenating the traditional style of French architecture, and by expanding the horizons of urban planning and designing, Le Corbusier gave greater prominence to an already well-known art form, the "international style."

His creations, similar in concept to those of American architect Frank Lloyd Wright, became France's best contributions to modern architecture. Among his most acclaimed structures, the Savoye House at Poissy-sur-Seine, an impressive building that looks like a polished sculpture and the Unité d'Habitation apartment house in Marseilles are two of his architectural masterpieces.

Despite efforts to decentralize, Paris remains the intellectual, political, economic, and financial center of France. Each president wants to leave his mark on the capital. Following this tradition, President François Mitterrand moved the Ministry of Finance out of the Richelieu Wing of the Louvre Palace, where it had been since 1871. The decision to alter the floor plan of the *Musée du Louvre* also called for a new entrance hall, designed by the American architect, I. M. Pei. His 71-foot-tall glass pyramid initially provoked a heated debate but quickly gained acceptance, once it was opened to the public for the 1989 bicentennial celebration of the French Revolution. On the Louvre's two hundredth anniversary in 1992, the *Musée du Louvre* became *Le Grand Louvre,* the largest museum in the world, with the expansion of its exhibit space by 60 percent. Other examples of what some have labeled the Mitterrand Style of Architecture are the *Arche de la Défense,* the *Opéra Bastille,* the *Institut du Monde arabe,* all of which express the desire of the French Government to explore new ideas and horizons through architecture.

Jean-Paul Sartre, whose writings have had a profound effect on the postwar generation throughout the world.

French Literature

Florence Steiner, Ph. D.

Trends in French Literature

French literature is in reality the history of man—man the individual, man a collective force to be reckoned with, man a creature to be governed, man a creature of God, man an instrument of fate, man a creator of his own destiny. From the beginning, French writers have tried to depict man and his society, at times using old themes in new ways, at times creating new themes that would inspire others. Certain trends in French literature are observable throughout the centuries.

One strain of French literature makes it a literature of the nobility. It was born of the ancients, just as the French language developed from Latin, Greek, and Celtic (or Gallic) components. The earliest epics deal with the Emperor Charlemagne, who is the central figure of the *Song of Roland*. The dramas of Pierre Corneille and Jean Racine (seventeenth-century playwrights) were based on myths and legends from the ancient Greeks but were portrayed in seventeenth-century style. Racine's *Andromaque* derives from the legend of the Trojan War and tells the story of Hector's widow and her struggle to save her son Astyanax. In *The Flies*, Jean-Paul Sartre has picked up another segment of the legend: Orestes was driven mad because he killed his mother, Clytemnestra, to avenge the death of his father, Agamemnon. Jean Giraudoux (twentieth century) treats the Trojan War in his *Tiger at the Gates.* Albert Camus' *Caligula* features a historical personage of Roman times and makes Caligula an "absurd" hero. This literature of the nobility is effective because it usually represents powerful people who go from a state of happiness to one of unhappiness.

A second element of French literature belongs to the middle class, or the bourgeoisie. This class of typically striving people is a good subject for the realistic novel and comedy. Molière sketched the bourgeoisie of the seventeenth century in his comedies. The novels of the nineteenth century also portrayed the middle class, and writers such as Stendhal showed the inspirations of the middle class in *The Red and the Black.* Honoré de Balzac depicted members of the middle class in his novels; one of them, *Father Goriot,* tells of the sufferings and sacrifices a father makes so that his daughters may live in an environment above his own. Other works which treat the middle class are Gustave Flaubert's *Madame Bovary* and Henry Becque's *Crows.* The latter shows what happens when a middle-class father dies leaving an incompetent widow and naïve daughters to manage his fortune and affairs.

A third theme is that of the lower classes. In ancient times the lower classes were thought to be the prime subject for comedy while the nobility was the more appropriate choice for tragedy. The lot of the lower classes was often portrayed in fable, since it was dangerous for the poor to counter the rich in writing, but nothing prevented them from telling tales where animals were the actors. Here the high born are subjects for ridicule and satire; the smaller, weaker animals triumph over the powerful and strong through their use of wit and cunning. The fox is the most frequent example of this, as he dupes the lion (representing the royal power) and the wolf (representing the lawyers and financial forces).

The Middle Ages were an age of the farce. In the *Farce of Master Pathelin* a lawyer, Pathelin, advises a shepherd how to dupe a cloth merchant to whom he owes money by pretending to be crazy. When the merchant demands payment, the shepherd pretends to be a sheep and answers *"Bè!"* Later, when Pathelin tries to collect his fee from the successful shepherd, he too is answered with *"Bè."*

François Villon was the poet of the poor, the justifier of those about to be hanged. He knew his topic well for he himself had been involved in burglary, theft, and murder and had been condemned to hang.

In addition to treating the three classes of society, French writers have commonly been reformers. Some have been legal reformers, such as Montesquieu in his *Spirit of the Laws,* or Jean-Jacques Rousseau, who wanted man to return to a simpler state of civilization. Some were men of science, such as Descartes, who wrote the *Discourse on Method.* Others were political critics, such as Voltaire, Diderot, and, again, Rousseau. Some criticized education and proposed reforms which furnished the base for many educational changes, especially in our own country.

French writers have been both borrowers and lenders. Renaissance poetry, inspired by Petrarch in Italy, became a model for poets in other countries. One seventeenth-century French dramatist (Corneille) borrowed a theme from a second-rate Spanish writer and gave the world a first-rate play *(Le Cid).* Dramatists from the seventeenth century to our own day have borrowed themes from the Greeks. The romantic writers of the nineteenth century borrowed from English and German authors and created outstanding works.

On the other hand, French writers have been, and are, widely imitated by non-French authors. Our own revolution was justified by ideas taken from Voltaire, Rousseau, and others. The French existentialist writers of the twentieth century are read and admired in many countries and have been translated into various languages.

French literature has also been a literature of poetry. This poetry has treated the traditional themes of love, nature, and death. A French poet, Saint-John Perse, won the Nobel Prize for literature in 1960. Charles Baudelaire sank to the depths of despair trying drugs and alcohol to produce new sensations, which were recorded in his famous *Flowers of Evil.* Arthur Rimbaud pursued the theory of the derangement of the senses in his poem *The Drunken Boat.* Pure lyricists, symbolists, surrealists, and contemporary poets pursue both known and unknown paths in French poetry.

Beginnings

It is difficult to tell just when a literature begins, for often it is of heritage of a preceding literature. So is it with French literature. All literature begins with language, and French grew out of the Roman conquest of Gaul (France) and the Latin language, transported into Gaul and blended with the native language. As is true of occupying armies, Roman soldiers mingled with the natives and left their language, Latin, imprinted on the land. But it was a Latin that changed and developed gradually, though all official documents continued to be written in Latin.

Middle Ages

It is in the famous Oaths of Strasbourg *(Serments de Strasbourg)* that we find the first recorded document in French. These were oaths of mutual support and alliance sworn by Louis the German and Charles the

Bald, grandsons of Charlemagne, against their brother Lothair. The oaths, sworn at Strasbourg in 842, were sworn in both French and German so that both armies could understand them, and the French text of this document marks the official beginning of French literature.

The Middle Ages in France saw a feudal society founded on two great principles: honor and faith. The first literary works of merit were epics, called in French *Chansons de Geste* ("Songs of Exploits"). The first recorded ones appeared about the eleventh century and were written to entertain pilgrims who undertook journeys to shrines. (There were few inns at that time and these pilgrims would often spend the night at a monastery.) Hardly any people were able to read and write in those days; so minstrels composed epic poems which they sang to the wayfarers. The minstrel was often forced to repeat great sections of his poem, and he had to have material that was lively and interesting. Just as with some present-day television programs, certain epics grew into serials, and we find various themes developed in different ways with sequels.

The most famous of these was the *Song of Roland,* reflecting the glory of Charlemagne. It contained elements of fantasy and miracle and outstanding feats of daring. Roland, a nephew of Charlemagne, was one of the famous twelve peers who lent the court of Charlemagne an aura of greatness. The peers were noted for their courage, initiative, and bravery. During the time that the Moors were occupying Spain, Charlemagne crossed the Spanish border to help combat the heretics, and the Moorish king, Marsile, pretended to be at the point of submitting to Charlemagne.

Ganelon, stepfather of Roland, hated his stepson because Roland was a greater warrior and more admired by Charlemagne than he. Roland, moreover, did not particularly care for his stepfather. Hence when an envoy had to be chosen to go into the dangerous Moorish country, Roland saw that his stepfather was given the dangerous task, and Ganelon swore to get even with his stepson. His mission accomplished, he entered into a pact with Marsile to plot Roland's death. Because Charlemagne's army, returning victoriously to France, had to pass through the narrow pass of Roncevaux, Ganelon arranged for Roland and the twelve peers to make up the rear guard, and he agreed with Marsile to bring his immense army to the pass. They allowed the main body of the army to go through unharmed, and only at the moment that Roland and the peers were preparing to enter did they attack.

Charlemagne had previously given Roland a horn to sound at the first hint of danger, but such was Roland's courage, or pride, that he refused to use the horn. It was only with his dying breath that he finally managed to blow it. Charlemagne, upon hearing it, said "Roland must be near death, otherwise he would not sound the horn." He turned about, found the treachery, exterminated the pagans, and brought back to France the bodies of Roland, his good friend, Olivier, and Archbishop Turpin. He decided that Ganelon's punishment would be death by being quartered: the man would have one hand tied to one horse, one hand to another horse, and each of his feet to two separate horses, and then they would charge in four different directions. Obviously, Roland had been avenged.

Much extravagance is found in this poem. At one point Archbishop Turpin killed a Moor by taking his sword and cutting the man so beautifully in two that one half of him fell to one side and one half of him fell to the other. Turpin was an archbishop who believed in God but also knew how to use the sword and his horse. Roland was a headstrong young man, admirable for his courage, commendable for his bravery, but lacking in wisdom and common sense. Olivier, his friend, and the wiser of the two, begged Roland to call Charlemagne via the horn. We hear again and again the term *la douce France* ("sweet France") as Roland and Olivier state their love of their country. We know that the war statistics aren't valid, for the poet says that for every French soldier killed, thousands of the enemy perished.

This naïve poem, written for a naïve people, nevertheless encompasses many epic proportions. There is a sensitivity and a sweep reminiscent of Homer. There is a contagion and a magic in the people involved. This is a literature of extremes: the "good guys" are on the side of Charlemagne; the "bad guys" are on the side of the Moors. This is a song of deeds, but through the deeds the characters emerge.

This type of literature was popular in France (as well as in Spain and other countries), and the *Song of Roland* is but one manifestation of the nature of the many epics popular at that time. This theme of Roland—his death, his loyalty to his peers, his acceptance of his lot—is reflected by later writers, the most famous of whom is Alfred de Vigny (nineteenth century).

In his poem *The Horn (Le Cor),* Vigny begins by saying: "O God, how sad is the sound of the horn in the evening from the depths of the forests." Vigny paints the picture of this valley at Roncevaux, of the loneliness and isolation of Roland at the moment he blows the horn. Clothing his sentiments in nineteenth-century lyricism, Vigny recalls the great moment of the blowing of the horn, the moment of Charlemagne and of Roland and of history.

Here we see an example of the French borrowing from themselves. This theme, which came from the early literature of France, appears again in different clothing. French authors are masters at taking an idea that was someone else's and giving it an originality, insight, and life that the original author never dreamed of. Vigny's poem is superior to the original in bringing into focus the solitude of Roland, the isolation of the peers.

Not all was honor and faith in the Middle Ages, however; there was also a lower literature born of and by the people, which showed itself in many different ways. Two favorite forms were the farce, whereby one person dupes another, and the *fabliaux,* verse narratives that treat some episode of a burlesque character. The famous *Novel of Renart,* really a collection of narratives in the form of verse, shows the fox, Renart, struggling with his traditional enemy, the wolf. Many have seen in this symbolism the underdog poorer classes struggling with the more powerful aristocracy, and it is usually the underdog who wins. This type of literature was necessary for the survival of the people who did not often win, and it, in turn, furnished literary thoughts and materials for the seventeenth-century writer, La Fontaine, who used the same animal characters in his famous fables. We also find many of the same tricks, treacheries, and underdog achievements in the plays of Molière (also in the seventeenth century).

So the Middle Ages embraced both noble literature and literature of the streets. It has been said, moreover, that men born of the highest estate could enjoy both types and men born of the lowest estate also could enjoy both. The mixture of the two is seen in the work of one great French poet of the Middle Ages, François Villon. This *gentleman* had an interesting life, and according to tradition escaped being hanged on several occasions only by the indulgence of the king. His poetry reflects dual tendencies of the Middle Ages, for he wrote poetry that is religious, expressing the faith of the Catholic church, and on the other hand, he wrote poems telling the sentiments of men about to be hanged. His famous *Ballad of the Hanged* tells those who are about to do the hanging to have Christian charity for those who are about to be hanged and to pray for them, not to have their hearts hardened against them. If they don't show pity, God may not, in his turn, have pity on them.

The Renaissance

After this atmosphere of faith and honor of the Middle Ages, the Renaissance came as a great contrast. The Renaissance accentuated man, put aside preoccupation with the afterlife, and took a hard look at what was going on. We see the birth of the theater in the church—in the reading of the gospel and answers by the choir. Next came religious pageants, put on in the churches. Later, when the roles of devils became intriguing, suddenly more devils than cherubs were involved, and the drama moved outside the church to the church steps, which formed the first modern stage.

The sixteenth century found France involved with wars in Italy when Francis I crossed into Italy to pursue military victory. However, he was conquered by what he found around him: beautiful gardens and statues, a revival of the learning of the ancients, a love of that which is beautiful in this world, the creation of a new type of architecture, a bursting forth of artists, painters, and sculptors whose one thought was to beautify life.

One of the great French literary figures of the Renaissance was François Rabelais, born at the end of the fifteenth century and raised by monks. He came to Lyon, not only having studied for the priesthood but also having studied medicine. He found, however, that medicine didn't pay; and scientific books didn't pay; so he began to edit old chronicles. He suddenly realized that the ideas expressed therein, and some of the extravagances, could be turned to good avail. So he began to write his first book, *Pantagruel,* and then its sequel, *Gargantua,* which tell the story of a dynasty of good giants. They are among the great satires of all time.

In book 1 of *Gargantua,* Rabelais describes the difference between the methods of education in the Middle Ages and the happy effects of the new education of the Renaissance. When the child is of age, he is first given to two men of the old school, who raise him in the old method. The result is that he becomes crazy, stupid, and a dreamer. His father, indignant over this, then gives him to another man, an excellent teacher who knows about the new methods and decides to take the youngster to Paris. During this time in Paris, war breaks out between Gargantua's father and the ambitious Picrochole, a neighbor. Only one monk, Frère Jean des Entommeures, is able to hold out against the encroacher. Gargantua returns and the enemy is powerless against this great giant, who frees his own men. After victory is assured, and in order to recompense Frère Jean, Gargantua builds the famous Abbey of Thélème, a magnificent castle where life is to be beautiful. The abbey will house both sexes and the motto will be "Do what you like."

Book 2 begins the series of adventures of Pantagruel—his education and his victorious wars. Book 3 is devoted to marriage. Should Panurge, a friend of Pantagruel, marry? He consults all sorts of people—poets, astrologers, monks, theologians, doctors, philosophers, judges—and finally goes to the oracle of the *Dive Bouteille* ("divine bottle"). Book 4 gives us the story of the journeys to this oracle and the adventures that occur along the way. Book 5 gives us the end of this fabulous trip. When they arrive at the oracle, only one word is spoken, the word *trinc*. Freely translated, this means "drink."

As we can see from the above, Rabelais enjoyed writing the books. He treated subjects that were dear to the hearts of his readers. The books, published in stages, contain much sordid realism, much comedy, and many passages of real literary merit, and won Rabelais a great reputation.

Another writer of this period was Pierre de Ronsard, whose love poems are popular today and who inspired the famous line: "Gather ye rosebuds while ye may for a time is swift a-flying." Ronsard was always encouraging young ladies to take advantage of the present day—to love him—pointing out to them that, with time, their beauty too would fade and they might not have this great opportunity again.

Seventeenth Century

The seventeenth century is most often called the century of Louis XIV, for it is his spirit which permeates and dominates the entire era, which was one of growing stability, the establishment of good taste, and balance and reason. After the Renaissance, which had enriched the French language, the language was in need of pruning and clarification, of stabilization. The people too, tired of war, sought political stability and wished to be sheltered against change. The great prime minister, Richelieu, therefore promised to do three things: (1) to reduce the power of the nobles, (2) to make the king all powerful in France, and (3) to make France all powerful in Europe. Richelieu, himself a man of letters, established the French Academy. His general patronage of the arts, however, at times proved to be a disadvantage since he tried his hand at writing and was on occasion jealous of those who were more successful.

This century is considered the period of the great flowering of French letters. It is at times thought contradictory that an age that produced stability and so many restraints could at the same time produce so many men of genius, writers who were endowed with talents in several different areas. René Descartes set the tone for the whole century with his *Discourse on Method*. His theory was that all passions should submit to reason, which should be the supreme judge of our actions. He further stated that tradition should also be submitted to reason, but he cautioned that we must not throw over that which we have known until, by means of reason, we have found something better with which to replace it.

Hence this century is also called the Age of Classicism because of the emphasis on moderation and reason. The century is also so rich in writers that it is difficult to single out one author for distinction.

Corneille

Corneille wrote dramas that created a struggle between love and honor.

His first success was a play entitled *Le Cid,* the subject of which he took from a Spanish author. But although the Spanish original was only mediocre, from this he created a very brilliant drama that is still popular in our time. Rodrigo, son of a nobleman, Don Diego, is a most eligible young bachelor at the court. He has fallen in love with Chimene, daughter of Count Gormas, who is the current military leader of the court. (Don Diego, the father of Rodrigo, had previously held this position.) The young prince needs a tutor, the older man gets the nod from the king, and the count is angered over what he considers a slight to his reputation. Don Diego suggests they settle the matter by marrying his son to the count's daughter and letting all end happily. But the count, angered, slaps Don Diego's face with his glove, an insult that could not be ignored. Rodrigo had never tried his luck in a duel, and no one questioned his bravery, but everyone begged him not to try to avenge his father. In a passionate monologue, Don Diego tells of the rage and fury that seized him since his old age prevents him from defending himself. Rodrigo, disheartened and grieving, and knowing that whichever way the fight turns out his love for Chimene is destroyed, goes forth to meet the count, hoping that he will be killed. But he is victorious, and Chimene pleads with the king to have Rodrigo killed since he had killed her father. She also tells her maid she still loves Rodrigo, but feels that her honor must match his and therefore she must demand his death.

A tragedy is avoided when the Moors invade the town and Rodrigo is called upon to lead the Spanish armies. Chimene is not to be put aside, however, and the king suggests that she demand a settlement by a duel. She picks Don Sanche, another of her suitors, as her champion. The king insists that she promise to marry the victor. Rodrigo wins, but spares the life of Don Sanche because the latter was wearing Chimene's colors and he could not harm anything connected with Chimene. Since her grief is so recent, the king allows her a year to dry her tears. During this time Rodrigo will carry the war to the Moors, and after that year they will marry.

The play was immediately successful but was attacked by the critics, and Richelieu encouraged the academy to judge *Le Cid* and make recommendations. Corneille accepted the recommendations; so his following plays have no happy endings. The hero or heroine gives all for honor and must live with the ensuing tragedy.

Racine

The other great dramatist of the seventeenth century is Jean Racine. Racine's plays were inspired by Greek and Roman myths and legends, but his characters are seventeenth-century Frenchmen. Racine's characters do not choose honor, however; they are passion-driven people and they follow their own will and desires, which combine to destroy them. Two of Racine's greatest plays are *Andromaque* and *Phèdre.*

Andromaque involves more than the eternal triangle; the play stems from the legend that, after the death of Hector and the Greek victory at Troy, Pyrrhus, Achille's son, had taken as his slaves Andromache, Hector's widow, and their small son Astyanax. According to ancient legend, Astyanax was thrown from a wall of Troy and killed, but Racine revived him and we find Andromache living as a slave in the court of Pyrrhus, who had burned Troy. At the beginning of the play, Andromache communicates her hatred of this man who is her master.

During the war, Pyrrhus had been betrothed to Hermione, daughter of Helen and Menelaus. Hermione has now come to wed Pyrrhus, but there are complications: Pyrrhus does not love Hermione. Instead, he has conceived a deep passion for Andromache and begs her to wed him and become his queen, not his slave. She refuses him, telling him that all she wants is to lead a quiet life remembering her only true love, Hector. Pyrrhus threatens to hand her son Astyanax to the Greeks to be killed, since the Greeks still hate and fear Hector's son. Orestes arrives, as ambassador of the Greeks, for the express purpose of taking Astyanax back. The plot is further complicated by the fact that Orestes is very much in love with Hermione and would like to marry her, but she disdains him since she loves Pyrrhus and expects to be queen. Orestes reminds her that Pyrrhus has delayed their wedding for some time and that this is an insult to her. At this moment Pyrrhus announces his determination to do the honorable thing. He will hand over Astyanax and he will marry Hermione since Andromache has refused him. However, as he passes by Andromache and she drops to one knee, he sees her beautiful shoulder, his rage softens, and once more Hermione's wedding is delayed. Hermione, impatient, tells Orestes that if he kills Pyrrhus she will wed him. Andromache's final act of sacrifice for her son is to marry Pyrrhus, but she intends to kill herself immediately after the ceremony. And Pyrrhus, bound by his marriage vows, will protect Astyanax for the rest of his life. In the temple at the wedding, Orestes kills Pyrrhus. Andromache gathers around her the followers of Pyrrhus and they slaughter the Greeks in revenge. Hermione, far from being pleased, throws herself on the body of Pyrrhus and covers Orestes with insults as she stabs herself, whereupon Orestes loses his reason (note the different reason for his madness in Sartre's *The Flies*).

Racine is more interested in studying the depths of passion than the struggle between honor and love. His characters, driven to destruction because of passion, are real and vivid personages, although they are at times thought to be controlled. Certainly Racine was a product of Port Royal, the seat of Jansenism.

The Counter-Reformation in France had provoked an awakening of faith and moral order in the Catholic church, and Port Royal became the seat of Jansenism, whose greatest exponent was Blaise Pascal. Pascal's greatest work is his *Thoughts (Pensées),* in which he tries to justify the Christian religion in short paragraphs of two, three, or four lines (some of them are longer). Some of his thoughts are responses to the dominant theory of reason: "It is the heart that feels God, not reason." Here's what faith is: "God sensitive to the heart, not to reason." Pascal, who was also a great mathematician, carried into his writings the clarity and organization of the man of geometry.

Molière

Another great exponent of reason—in addition to Descartes—was Molière, the pseudonym of Jean-Baptiste Poquelin. Molière, unlike Corneille and Racine, wrote comedies based on the Italian equivalent of vaudeville. His plays contain stock characters and his plots come from various sources (from the ancient comedians, the Italians, and the French), but he reworked the plots in terms of the seventeenth century. Observing the happenings at court, he saw that Louis XIV wanted to transfer the balance of political power to the middle classes so that he could reduce the power of the nobles. As the middle class acquired more and more money, it tried to emulate the nobles—to have the same manner of dress and living the nobles had adopted—but, alas, it did not have the background and the taste to do so. Many of Molière's comedies try to show the fallacy of such action.

Molière had a young wife, whom he married in his later years, but he was unhappy in this marriage. His plays, therefore, often contain a young girl whom her father wishes to marry to an older man she doesn't love. Molière became the champion of these young girls. In his plays he urges fathers to reconsider, telling them that daughters have means of revenge that they have never considered. In each Molière play there is one person who represents the voice of reason as the comedy becomes more extravagant.

One of his best-loved plays is the *Middle-Class Gentleman.* Monsieur Jourdain is a cloth merchant who has become wealthy and who now wants to make his way in the world of the life of the court. He sends for his tailor, and at the beginning of the play we find him trying on a ridiculous costume which he considers elegant. Although he is married, has two children, and a very practical middle-class wife, he aspires to the love of a certain marquise. But he really doesn't love her; he just wants to have the opportunity to write poetry to her. Of course—since he doesn't know how to write poetry—he sends for a teacher to help him learn how to write and how to speak. He wants to learn all the beautiful things that one needs to know. He is delighted to find that he has been speaking prose all his life, and that all that is not poetry is prose and all that is not prose is poetry. He also sends for a dancing master and tries to learn how to dance. The family servant, Nicole, points out to him the ridiculous nature of his actions. When he sends for a fencing master, she says that she can perform better than he, and she soon proves that she can in a very funny scene.

M. Jourdain, like other Molière heroes, has a daughter of marriageable age who wants to marry a certain Cleonte, who is not a noble but who is a good member of the middle class. M. Jourdain does not want to allow this marriage since he aspires to greater heights for his daughter. The family decides to play a trick on him by dressing Cleonte as the son of a great Turk and by having a festival. During the festival, M. Jourdain is told that the son of the great Turk has become enamored of his daughter and wishes to marry her. Delighted, he allows the marriage to none other than Cleonte.

As in the case of many other plays, this one was written at the desire of the king, who wanted a ballet that would have a Turkish quality about it. So Molière wrote a play that could include this type of performance.

The success of Molière's comedies certainly does not depend on the plots; it is rather his treatment of character and his knowledge of human beings—their weaknesses and lack of proportion—that make his plays great. In each of them one sees a character carried to excess, just as the heroes and heroines of tragedy were carried to excess. In the comedies, however, reason is sometimes able to balance the excesses.

Eighteenth Century

Louis XIV was able to both foster and control good taste and the cultivation of the beautiful. He built the palace of Versailles, to which he invited the nobility, and for their enjoyment he presented the best music, ballet, and theater of his century. At his death, however, a new wind was blowing. There was no strong leader to take his place; so the people, discontent over the amount of money spent on Louis' wars and on building Versailles, began to protest. New literary forms, especially the essay and the novel, came to express these complaints.

The eighteenth century, the century of prose, produced three outstanding writers and philosophers: Montesquieu, Voltaire, and Rousseau. Montesquieu's *Spirit of the Laws* made great contributions to sociology, experimental science, and politics. He discusses three types of government—the republic, monarchy, and autocracy—as well as the qualities which underlie them. He maintains that it is virtue which underlies the republican form of government, honor which sustains the monarchy, and fear which upholds autocracy.

Voltaire

Voltaire was one of the greatest literary spirits of France. Often exiled for speaking out, for satirizing that which shouldn't be satirized, Voltaire nevertheless was responsible in large part for both the American and the French revolutions. He denounced abuses, attacking governments and religions alike. These were two institutions which had not been previously attacked with any great vigor. Exiled to England, he became an admirer of the English form of government. He later went to Prussia, to the court of Frederick the Great, but soon became disillusioned.

A poet and a historian, he could not accept blind destiny and the theory that all is for the best. He stood for tolerance and he used irony as a weapon against those who were intolerant. His greatest creation was *Candide,* in which he attacks optimism by telling the story of Candide, a very fine, innocent, naïve, young man who lived in a castle and fell in love with the baron's daughter, Mademoiselle Cunegonde. Both had been taught by an excellent tutor, Pangloss. One day, however, the baron caught Candide kissing Cunegonde, and Candide was dismissed from the best of all possible castles most unceremoniously. Thereupon he underwent a series of adventures. He went into the army, deserted, and went to Holland, where he met Pangloss, and they journeyed together to Lisbon, arriving as a great earthquake occurred. They survived but were seized by the Inquisition. Pangloss was hanged (but did not die) and Candide received a hundred lashes, but he met Cunegonde, who also had undergone a series of adventures. Together they went to America, but there Candide lost Cunegonde again, killed her brother, visited Eldorado, returned, and found that Cunegonde was a slave and had become horribly ugly. But Pangloss was still sure that everything was going to work out all right. Candide saved the whole group, but another brother of Cunegonde still did not think him good enough to marry her. Nevertheless, marry her he did, and they established themselves on a little farm where Candide decided that he would devote his life to making his garden grow and to no other philosophical end. *Candide* has been set to music by Leonard Bernstein, but there are also many other poems and musical treatments which have been published.

Rousseau

The third great writer of the eighteenth century is Jean-Jacques Rousseau. Rousseau had a Protestant background, but his system of thought influenced political and educational thinking in Catholic France. All of his philosophy is based on one idea: that nature made man good and civilization made him bad. The basis of civilization is property, which is bad, and the mark of civilization is the development of the sciences and the arts, which also is bad. Nevertheless, civilization can ennoble man. We must first remake ourselves as natural men, without throwing out that which ennobles civilized man. In education, he wanted that which was natural for children, not that which was imposed. *Le Contrat social, La Nouvelle Heloïse,* and *Emile* are three of his most important works.

Nineteenth Century

From the works of these thinkers grew the revolt that culminated in the French Revolution at the end of the eighteenth century. The nineteenth century is born of the revolution. Alfred de Musset said that, during the wars of the empire, a new generation was conceived between battles and was raised to the sound of drums. The young had known no other life; they were living between two worlds: the past which was gone forever and the future which had not yet come. The revolution brought with it a dissolution of the great estates belonging to the nobility and the church. The middle class, seizing upon the opportunity, bought parts of these estates and reassembled new ones.

The nineteenth century began on a glorious, unified tone as Napoleon, gaining control of France after the revolution, led France to the pinnacle of territorial conquest. Then, with his fall, France floundered.

The literature of the nineteenth century is twofold in that two great movements were born of it: romanticism and realism. Romanticism is a product of war. It is an escape literature, a literature that goes back to and was inspired in the Middle Ages, a literature that is preoccupied with the individual, a literature that seeks the exotic. Melancholy prevails throughout. This melancholy, called *mal du siècle,* rejects the order of the classical period. Romanticism prefers to sing the lyric song of the individual and the personality of each author shines through. It is sentimental, it is descriptive, it is emotional. It breaks the rules of the classics and rejects the cult of antiquity. It proclaims the Middle Ages and foreign literatures, especially Shakespeare and Goethe.

Victor Hugo

One of its greatest exponents was Victor Hugo, poet, dramatist, and novelist, who showed real talent in all three areas. His great masterpiece, *Les Misérables,* has been translated into many languages and is enjoyed by people throughout the world. The central character is Jean Valjean, a convict who has been freed after nineteen years of penal servitude (he was originally condemned for having stolen a loaf of bread to feed his starving nephew). Because of an ill-advised action, he can be sent back to the galleys, but under the name of Monsieur Madeleine he tries to rehabilitate himself. He becomes interested in all of the unfortunates and is kind to an unfortunate woman, Fantine, and her child, Cosette.

Then M. Madeleine learns that the police have arrested a man they believe is the former convict, Jean Valjean, and he suffers a terrible conflict within himself. Giving himself up to save the innocent man, he is sent back the the galleys; but then he escapes. He rescues Cosette from her cruel foster parents and both of them go to Paris. Cosette now believes Jean Valjean to be her father. They manage to evade a suspicious police inspector and find shelter in a convent. Cosette grows up and a young man, Marius, of good family, falls in love with her and courts her despite Jean Valjean's protests. One day, going to the barricades, Jean finds young Marius, who is wounded, puts him on his shoulders, and saves him, carrying him out by means of the sewers. Once Marius is cured, the marriage takes place and Jean Valjean gives Cosette a generous dowry. Then he tells Marius who he really is and of his desire to live a better life. Marius is shocked to learn that his father-in-law is an ex-convict, and Jean Valjean dies slowly because he doesn't have Cosette near him any longer.

Flaubert

In contrast to this type of novel is Gustave Flaubert's *Madame Bovary*. Like Hugo, Flaubert displays elements of romanticism in his works, but he represents not only romanticism but realism—and realism carried to naturalism. If realism is painting life as it is and not as it should be, naturalism tries to submit life to a laboratory examination. It tries to remove all traces of the author's personality from the work. It wants the novel to be objective and impersonal.

Madame Bovary is a work of minute observation in which each adjective, each noun is chosen carefully. Flaubert tells the story of Emma, the daughter of a Norman peasant reared in a convent and a lover of romantic tales who sees herself leading a life of love and pleasantness. In order to escape life on the farm (to which she has returned), she marries Charles Bovary, a country doctor, but she soon discovers the mediocrity of this narrow, limited man and becomes tremendously bored. Trying to carry her romantic ideas into reality, she becomes the mistress of several men. Then, falling into debt, she tries to borrow money but is unsuccessful. When a creditor menaces her, she seeks out a former lover to get money from him, but again is unsuccessful. Finally, realizing the situation in which she has placed herself, and fearing to reveal to her husband the debts she has contracted, she takes poison. Flaubert's Emma

Bovary is an unbalanced romantic who is unable to cope with her environment.

Poets

Hugo, along with three other romantic poets, Alphonse de Lamartine, Alfred de Vigny, and Alfred de Musset, also made great contributions to poetry at the beginning of the century. At the end of the century, symbolism appeared in poets like Paul Verlaine, Arthur Rimbaud, and Stéphane Mallarmé. The great poet of naturalism is Charles Baudelaire. Haunted by his ideas of death, sensuality, and mysticism, he was the link between romanticism and symbolism. He wanted to experience that which is new, that which man had never experienced or tried before. His great work, *Flowers of Evil,* reflects his experiences.

Twentieth Century

The twentieth century has also produced great novelists, poets, and dramatists. A great novelist of the early twentieth century is Marcel Proust, who was preoccupied with time and trying to recreate the past. He wrote a series of novels entitled *In Search of Time Past.* André Gide was interested in the individual and his personality, be it psychological or moral. One of his great works, *The Pastoral Symphony,* is the story of a minister who takes a blind girl to live with him and his family. Through her physical blindness the reader becomes aware of the minister's spiritual blindness, as little by little he falls in love with the girl. His own son, who also loves the girl, tries to reveal this to him, but unsuccessfully. Two other great novelists of the twentieth century are Jean-Paul Sartre and Albert Camus, both of whom wrote not only novels but dramas and essays as well.

Sartre is first of all a philosopher, and one of the fathers of existentialism. According to Sartre, God doesn't exist, and man comes into an absurd world which has only him as a reason for being. At his birth, man is nothing but a body joined irrevocably to a consciousness. This consciousness is perceptible only when something fills it; otherwise it is empty. Nevertheless, man has one major attribute, freedom of choice. Man is absolutely free to build his life as he wishes without taking any notice of divinity, which does not exist. His life will be no more and no less than the total sum of all his choices, but with each choice come certain responsibilities. We are only what we make ourselves; hence Sartre's formula: Existence precedes essence and creates it.

Camus

Albert Camus, winner of the Nobel Prize in 1957, said, as did Sartre and others, that man is born a stranger in an alien world—in a world that he does not understand and that does not understand him. This world is absurd. That he is born condemned to die is the only thing of which he can be certain.

Camus' great novel *The Stranger* is an example of this doctrine in action. Mersault is a sensuous man, very conscious of the sea, the air, the odors around him, but very unconscious of the human beings around him—except for those who touch his life directly. He doesn't play the game according to the rules; he doesn't give the pat answers that people expect of him. One day, in self-defense, he kills an Arab, but because he had exhibited strange behavior at his mother's funeral—he had not wept—the jury was prejudiced against him, thinking him a cold, indifferent person who killed ruthlessly.

As a matter of fact, at the moment Mersault fired the gun at the Arab the sun had blinded him and, though he pulled the trigger five times, he had not realized what he was doing. He doesn't repent, beat his breast, and go through the motions that are expected of him; so he is condemned to death. It is only after he is condemned that he experiences the sense of freedom that is the peculiar to the existentialist.

Now he sees himself in true perspective. He knows that the world is dear to him, that he has built his life on a series of choices and that those choices still interest him. He finally declares his freedom when a priest visits him and asks him to believe in God. Mersault tells the priest that he doesn't know what interests him but that he knows what doesn't interest him. He knows that his life as he has led it is real to him and what the priest is talking about is not. He knows that he is like other men, since all are condemned to die, but he also knows that he is different. His life has been real, his approaching death is real, and once he has lost all hope of an appeal he can open himself to the tender indifference of the world.

Beckett

One of the most important plays of our time is Samuel Beckett's *Waiting for Godot*. (Beckett, an expatriate Irishman, lived in France and wrote in both French and English.) Like Camus, Beckett is concerned with man's fate and his ability to live with this fate. If Camus sees man as born to die, as living in this world yet condemned to death, Beckett sees him condemned to wait, and waiting brings with it a sense of boredom. All Beckett's art, theatrical skill, and use of language converge to create this boredom. In order to highlight the emptiness of life, the stage is practically devoid of scenery. (One tree on a country road is all the author recommends for scenery.) The main characters are two tramps, Estragon and Vladimir, who are waiting for Godot. These men are not heroes in the traditional sense; indeed, they are repellent. Suffering from hunger, they eat turnips, radishes, and occasional carrots, and beg chicken bones from one Pozzo, who interrupts their reverie. During their waiting they are bored with each other, even repulsed by each other, but they decide that they have been together too long to part and that they don't want to face the loneliness of being separated.

Appearances to the contrary, they are for the most part human and humane. They are interested in man and in his suffering, recognizing their own suffering in another's misery. Pozzo too is drawn into the mystery of Godot and waits with them, confessing that he would be happy to meet Godot.

Godot never comes. At the end of each act, however, he sends a messenger to assure the two tramps that he will arrive. The messenger, a young boy, gives a few details about Godot: he has a beard, and the boy thinks it is white. Estragon finally proposes dropping Godot, but Vladimir counters: "He'd punish us. Everything's dead but the tree."

Why are the two waiting for Godot? We never learn. At the end of the play, however, after they consider hanging themselves but desist for lack of a good bit of rope, Vladimir says: "We'll hang ourselves tomorrow. Unless Godot comes." Estragon asks; "And if he comes?" to which Vladimir replies: "We'll be saved." Perhaps, then, Godot represents salvation, either God's salvation or the existentialist answer of man's salvation of himself.

Beckett's art includes the use of certain techniques from vaudeville. The two tramps seem a bit reminiscent of the tradition of clowns. The histrionics of Pozzo and Lucky, his slave, involve several old tricks, such as the master berating the loyal servant, and the servant kicking those who would help him. There is also a sudden reversal of roles as Vladimir and Estragon sympathize momentarily with Pozzo. So we wait through Act I, and we wait through Act II (in reality a repetition of Act I), and finally we realize that waiting is the crucial experience of the Beckett character. It involves enduring the world's nonsense, its absurdity, without clear hope of immediate or direct help. [1]

Perhaps the most succinct description of French literature, as distinct from others, is given by André Gide in his *Prétextes:* "There are moors harsher than the moors of Brittany; pastures greener than the pastures of Normandy; rocks redder than the rocks around Arles; beaches more blue-green than the beaches of the Channel, more azure than the beaches of the Riviera. But France is all that at the same time. And the French genius is, for this reason, not only moors, only tillages, only forests, only shadows, only light—but one that organizes and keeps in one harmonious balance all those diverse elements."

---

1. Frederick J. Hoffman, *Samuel Beckett: The Language of Self* (New York: Dutton, 1964), p. 151.

Founder and director of the *Institut de Recherche et Coordination Acoustique/ Musique,* Pierre Boulez is one of the most controversial figures in contemporary music.

French Music

Monica Rogers

When a major television network was planning a program to be called "The Twenty-First Century," there was a search, as there always is, for a musical theme with relevance—something with a *right sound.* The perfect combination of aural effects was located in a composition with the futuristic title "Intercelestial Tabulator." The recording had been realized in Paris, and the liner notes describe the record as "Futurism, busy with exciting tempo."

This description might serve as well for certain trends that are finding expression in French music of today, for the music scene in France reveals much that is contemporary and much that has relevance because of the past. Anyone thinking the current rush toward change is exclusive to this age has only to look at past periods of music history to discover a working meaning of cultural relevance.

The Ars Nova

Somewhere around the year 1325, the French composer, poet, and theorist, Philippe de Vitry (1291-1361), wrote a work entitled *Ars Nova* (the "new art" or "new technique"). The only novelty in this particular work was Philippe's description of a new way of dividing and measuring time, the term *ars nova* was so appropriate that it has come to be used to encapsulate the musical style that prevailed in France during the first half of the fourteenth century.

As the thirteenth century had been an era of stability and unity, the fourteenth was one of change and variety. Everyone "did his own thing," but shifting habits is a slow process. At least, so it was in that century—the process was re-emphasis, not a sudden reversal. Many tendencies and traits characteristic of the fourteenth century had appeared before 1300, and many features of the thirteenth century persisted for a long time after that date. Every age preserves and develops some elements from the past, but it is also inevitable that it rejects others; whether the result in any given instance is an improvement, or the reverse, is a question that cannot always be decided with complete objectivity.

The musicians of the early fourteenth century were conscious of striking out a new path. The currents seem familiar: the "ancients" (the thirteenth-century musicians) were against the claims of the "moderns." The issues were (1) the modern acceptance of duple or imperfect division of time values in addition to the traditional triple or perfect division; and (2) the rhythmic and notational complexities of the modern music which resulted from the use of both perfect and imperfect division and from the use of short note-values. In other words, the "moderns" were saying the "beat" had to change.

Rhythmic subtlety, at times carried to unbelievable proportions, was indeed the most obvious point in which the music of the fourteenth century differed from that of the earlier period; but other, and equally important, contrasts emerged. Intervals (thirds and sixths) occurred more often in consonant (pleasant sounding) positions (that is, on strong beats), though the final sound was still always a unison, octave, or open fifth. These intervals moved in parallel motion; on the other hand, parallel fifths, unisons, and octaves appeared less frequently.

The thirteenth century was the last great unified medieval musical period for most of the music created was based on rhythmic variation. The fourteenth century, though still medieval, was an era of relatively rapid change. Much of its music sounds experimental and tentative. Some, however, sounds overdone—like the manners of its knightly patrons. Most of what has come down to us in manuscript was composed for the pleasure of aristocratic and cultivated listeners or amateurs. However, contemporary pictures and writings of the time show that the practice of music, both vocal and instrumental, was widespread among all social classes. The leading composer of the period was Guillaume de Machaut. He was one of the first composers to make use of isorhythm (same rhythm). He also perfected the *ballade* style of composition. He will always be noted, however, for creating the most famous musical composition of that period, the *Messe de Notre Dame* (Mass of Our Lady)—the first complete setting of the Mass Ordinary.

The Renaissance contrapuntists wrote note-against-note music derived from the single-line chant of the Gallican plainsong, which had been used in France until the time of Charlemagne. By the sixteenth century, its composers had acquired such masterful skill that vocal counterpoint became a stylistic science. Their ability to imitate sounds in order to describe things can be understood in *La Bataille (Battle of Marignan)* and *Le Chant des Oiseaux (Awakening of the Birds)* by Clément Janequin. Claude Le Jeune (c. 1530-c. 1600), Guillaume Costeley (1531-1606), and Claude de Sermisy (c. 1490-1562), are other names associated with the period. Western music until the sixteenth century was modal, that is, it used only the tones of the basic diatonic scale (the white keys of the piano), and generally, it had a single melodic line, unaccompanied—the Gallican plainchant mentioned before, or the secular songs of the troubadours and trouvères. The "times" were changing again.

After the Sixteenth Century

The age of Louis XIV saw the gradual abandonment of the ancient scales and a concentration on the ordinary major and minor. Music began to be composed around the fixed tonal intervals of keyboard instruments. With the tempered scale, a division of the octave into twelve equal tones and twenty-four half-tones, twelve major and twelve minor, composers could move from one key to another to create effects of greater tension and more complex harmony. There was a principal tone (key-feeling, tonal center) around which the music was organized. Loyalty to the tonal center (defined as a sound with pitch, duration, intensity, and timbre) was important. Melody and harmony (the pleasant relationship of tones simultaneously sounded) remained the important factors of composition. Further changes involved the outside (highest and lowest) voices.

Melody was given importance over its accompaniment, whereas the previous century had given all parts the same importance. It was not as important in sound—it didn't burst forth bravely—as it is today in modern music, but it was changing. In spite of some excellent writing by the seventeenth-century composers, the vocal line remained somehow backward in expressiveness. The treble was very ornate; it seemed bogged down by the public taste. It aimed to please or amuse, rather than discover a way to express musical thought. The bass line was emphasized. By the late Baroque, it was customary for a composer to establish a driving rhythmic pattern at the beginning of the composition or movement and to hold to this basic pattern throughout. Instrumental works and pieces for the organ showed conciseness and charm—and an occasional noble thought.

In the opera, the composer did not dare to translate into music the feeling embodied in the play. Born in Italy, Jean Baptiste Lully (1632-1687) was the most famous of French operatic composers. He learned to adapt himself entirely to the prevailing fashion. He was able to blend the colorful ballet and the classical French tragedy into a form called *tragédie lyrique* ("tragedy in music").

In the latter part of Louis XIV's reign, François Couperin (1668-1733) was called upon to write intimate, quiet music. It was completely French in spirit: Sophisticated, witty, deceptively simple and clear.

Widening France's Musical Horizon

The third period of musical change in France occurred in *romanticism*. Here again, the tendency was indicated in the preceding century. In the eighteenth century, Jean-Philippe Rameau predicted a future direction for music in his theoretical writing *Treatise on Harmony Reduced to its Natural Principles*. It was an important work because it summed up and clarified methods of composers of the preceding generations as well as pointing to the future: Musical style was to come through harmony, not counterpoint.

The philosophers also foresaw the day when music would become a more powerful art through the use of expressive means and a recognition of human feeling. The period that prepared the revolution of 1789 set forth this idea in connection with its appeal for freedom and rights. This appeal led to the production of joyful and enthusiastic music. In keeping with this feeling, the operatic works of Christoph Willibald Gluck (1714-1787) had a considerable influence, and this was true despite the fact that in the famous Quarrel of the Buffoons* it was the Italian school that triumphed. But the French musicians did not at first grasp the true purpose of Gluck's reforms—and surely not the theoretical discussions he inspired. They had forgotten Rameau's words—and it should have been clear that his technique was necessary to develop a French school. One important feature in this century was a constant public demand for making music popular, in keeping with the revolutionary principles. This last tendency produced the great heroic and national songs—the *Chant du départ* of Etienne Méhul (1763-1817) and Joseph Rouget de Lisle's *Marseillaise* (1792). These were born of exceptional circumstances.

*The traditionalists who adhered to the precepts of classical Baroque opera clashed with the advocates of *opera buffa* or light opera (usually comic). Gluck had sought to combine the best of both.

Mention should also be made of the charming and intelligent works of André Grétry (1742–1813), the merit of Méhul's *Joseph,* and the operas and oratorios of Jean-François Le Sueur (1760-1837).

It was not until the appearance of Hector Berlioz (1803-1869), in the third decade of the nineteenth century, that we find a solid musical structure, animated with a new and characteristic melody, supported by expressive harmony and rhythmical inventiveness. This extraordinary musician and man of genius had to devise nearly all his musical resources, writing, while still at the Paris Conservatoire, the overture, *Les Francs-Juges.*

Berlioz wrote works of large dimension and vigorous sonority which were essentially French. One should notice his characteristic of measure and proportion, which is not incompatible with large-scale works. He was brought up on Virgil, and the traces of this feeling for antiquity are to be found in *Les Troyens* and *L'Enfance du Christ.*

Berlioz is our near ancestor, because with him the modern musical world is already in being. His works reveal the emotion aroused by the mystery of things which the nineteenth century taught us to love: the sea, the mountains, the night, the spectacle of nature. Other works that reveal his genius are *Harold in Italy* (a symphony which is almost a viola concerto), *Romeo and Juliet* (a dramatic symphony), *Symphonie Fantastique,* (a literary symphony in which he expanded descriptive elements, it further illustrates the development of a suite into a symphony). French composers have never completely recovered from his influence. He is the creator of the symphonic poem and the liberator of harmony, rhythm, and development.

César Franck (1822-1890) was the first after Berlioz to see into music far and wide, and his long concentration on the inner life was nothing but a seeking after the perfection of technique to express his thoughts. An adopted Frenchman (of Belgian ancestry), he was the strongest figure in instrumental music, giving his contemporaries the principle of cyclicism (repeating themes, unchanged, throughout a symphony). The harmonic language he used came from the doodling that he did at the organ, developing a thick orchestral sound that is most characteristic of the quality of French organs. As a French Wagnerite, he brought a subtlety of expression to French music—exemplified in his *Symphonic Variations,* which are a mixture of piano concerto and non-virtuoso symphonic thought.

French art songs, or *mélodies,* are another musical *genre* that has received staunch defense from historians. The rise and fall of the French language suggested the characteristic shape of the vocal line. Though this style began with Gounod and Franck, it was more important in the next generation with Ernest Chausson, Henri Duparc, and Gabriel Fauré. This sort of music is without a doubt the most faithful rendering of the sentiments uttered by the poets. A good portion of Fauré's work consists of admirable melodies written to the lyrics of Paul Verlaine. The size of these works does not affect their greatness. A beautiful song is worth more than a volume of tedious sonatas—it would be a grave error to overlook the charm of this musical form.

As far as opera was concerned at that time, Paris became the mecca of all operatic composers. It was a rather French-Italian brand of grand opera, because the leading composers of this period were from other countries. They were apparently fascinated with Paris as a place to live and to work. The fact that Paris also had the grandest opera house in the world also accounted for their love for the city. The works of Spontini *(La Vestale),* Rossini *(Guillaume Tell),* and Meyerbeer *(Robert le Diable* and *Les Huguenots)* were heard. There was also *opéra comique.* But the operas that were making the greatest impression were those that were by French composers: Charles Gounod's *Faust* (1869), Georges Bizet's *Carmen* (1875), and Jules Massenet's *Manon* (1884). One aspect of this period was the rise of French nationalism in music.

Emmanuel Chabrier could profit from foreign influences without endangering his own nationalistic tendencies, and for this he became a great influence on twentieth-century composers. Chabrier (1841-1894) was a truly original talent, to whom succeeding musicians owed more than they knew. He was a typical artist, speaking and writing as he liked. His melody was alive, his harmonic inventions were genuine.

Other composers who are grouped in this period include Camille Saint-Saëns *(Danse macabre),* whose biblical opera *Samson et Dalila* (1877) is his most important work, and Vincent d'Indy's *Symphony on a French Mountaineer's Song,* which brought together symphonic application of traditional music, piano concerto and thematic metamorphosis. With the exception of César Franck, however, the French composers demonstrate the fundamental unromanticism of French music, striving more for classic ideals of elegance. This may have been one reason why France progressed so quickly to anti-romantic aims in the twentieth century.

There was further the establishment of the National Society for French Music, in order to retain a national identity after France's defeat in the Franco-Prussian War. There was also a conscious effort to recover the characteristics of excellent national music from folksong and a revived past: Rameau and the sixteenth-century composers. In 1894, the Schola

Cantorum was founded in Paris—the result of all these activities produced results of prime importance to music everywhere.

Claude Debussy's Revolution

There are three works that revolutionized twentieth-century music: *Five Orchestra Pieces,* Opus 16 (1909) by Arnold Schoenberg, *The Rite of Spring* (1912) by Igor Stravinsky, and *Jeux* (1913) by Claude Debussy. The last work is growing into this role because of the work of Pierre Boulez. During the 1960's, performances by various orchestras that Pierre Boulez conducted without a score gave proof that *Jeux* was as sure and strong a masterpiece as the other revolutionary works—and as much a landmark as Debussy's own *La Mer* and *Prelude to the Afternoon of a Faun or Syrinx.*

Of all the musicians who ever lived, Claude Debussy (1862-1918) was one of the most original and most adventurous. For every sort of voice and instrument, he made music that differed radically from the common practice of his predecessors, Rameau to Fauré. His music has won a permanent place in the repertory of every kind of performer and performing group. His achievement is unique.

The influence of his style spread quickly throughout the Western world. It freed his compatriots in France from their obsession with Beethoven and Wagner and enabled France to replace Germany and Austria, at least temporarily, as the center of attraction for the musicians in England, America, Russia, and other distant countries. Debussy's influence spread affecting all forms of music. It spread into churches, schools, ballrooms, as well as theaters and concert halls. Not only his music, but his ways of thinking in melodies and tone colors, were copied. Without knowing his name or the title of his *Clair de Lune,* everyone knows the sounds and patterns of Debussy.

Some of his significant works should be listed, and though opinions differ, these cannot be overlooked: The first is *The Afternoon of a Faun.* He also wrote one completed opera: *Pelléas et Mélisande,* which has enjoyed a recent revitalization by Pierre Boulez. In 1912, he composed a flute solo *(Syrinx)* to be used as incidental music for the scene of the death of Pan in a play by Gabriel Mourey, *Psyché. Jeux,* Debussy's last, most difficult piece for orchestra, with scenario by Nijinsky, was a masterpiece in the history of dancing. *Etudes* (1915) for piano, is considered the best matched set of pieces that he wrote.

Debussy opened up the music of Western Europe to the music of the rest of the world. He absorbed a profound influence from the Indonesian *gamelan* and made use of Afro-American ragtime. But Debussy established no new conventions, founded no school, and declined to prophesy the future of music. His work, in spite of its vast influence, is modest, slender, and personal. It does not rank with that of Bach or Mozart or Wagner in quantity or scope, yet he revolutionized a century.

The history of Debussy's revolution is then but a natural episode in the evolution of musical art. The lapse of time enables us to measure his effect, and we now understand more clearly than in the heat of contemporary debate that elegance in style does not exclude musical construction or strong and intense expression. These are some of the factors involved in this long process of emancipation:

1. Modern composition won freedom from rules of harmony which prohibited certain chord progressions.
2. New views of tonality and modulation were achieved. Modulations were written with greater freedom, and pieces did not hold to the tonal center as in times past.
3. There was freedom in rhythms.
4. There was freedom in symphonic style.
5. There was the acceptance of a new principle: the greatness of a work is not measured by its duration in time, nor by its volume, nor by the compelling beat of its rhythm; but by its beauty, and its idea.

Between the impact of Debussy and the group of composers who emerged after World War I should come the work of two native French musicians, Albert Roussel and Charles Koechlin.

Roussel's work appeared relatively late, because he trained first for the navy and only took up music in his thirtieth year. He studied under d'Indy at the Schola Cantorum, taught there, went again on his travels, and in 1909 produced this three symphonic poems, *Evocations*.

Charles Koechlin's output is practically unknown, and, in fact, little of his music has so far been published; performances of his works are even more rare. His champions, though few, are dedicated. His orchestral skill has won great respect from his colleagues. *Las Bandar-Log* is a brilliant and splashy orchestral suite that Koechlin began in 1939 at the age of seventy-two. He completed the work two years later.

An article by Henri Collet happened to group six French composers together in this title, *Les Six and Erik Satie*. They are always mentioned as the French Six or the Paris Six. This postwar school shared some features in common with *L'Ecole d'Arcueil,* and the neoclassical. Deriving, in the main, from Chabrier and to a lesser extent from Erik Satie, these young composers exploited the parody style. Influenced by Stravinsky and often commissioned to work for Diaghilev, they wrote ballets based on popular music hall tunes, of simple and insistent rhythm, scored either for jazz band or for combinations of instruments accidentally grouped. To lend sophistication, contrapuntal effects and ultramodern harmonies were added to the mixture. Melody was avoided as likely to suggest sentiment.

Of the Paris Six, Georges Auric, Louis Durey, Darius Milhaud, Arthur Honegger, Francis Poulenc, and Germaine Tailleferre, Auric and Poulenc produced their chief works in ballet form between 1917 and 1924. Milhaud and Honegger later broke away and devoted themselves to music apart from the ballet. Later, three of this group became identified as exponents of Neo-Classicism in France: Arthur Honegger *(King David, Pacific #231)*, Darius Milhaud *(la Création du monde)*, and Francis Poulenc *(Le Dialogue des Carmélites)*.

In 1936 there was a group founded in Paris called *La Jeune France.* Not having a common philosophy, its unity derived from general aspirations and tendencies. It was a reaction against the abstract tendencies of middle-European composers as represented in the *Triton,* Paris' society of contemporary music. The following manifesto, printed in the program of the first concert (June 3, 1936) had this declaration: "As living conditions become more and more hard, mechanical and impersonal, music must bring its spiritual fortitude and its generous reactions to those who love it. *La Jeune France,* reviving a term created by Berlioz a long time ago, pursues the road upon which the master once took his course. . . . At each concert . . . several works characteristic of some interesting trend . . . . will be performed." It seems to be an interesting way to protest.

Of this group, Olivier Messiaen became a leading figure. During his captivity as a prisoner of war at Görlitz, Silesia, in 1941, he composed a *Quartet for the End of Time,* scored for violin, clarinet, violincello, and piano. Of his works composed since that period in his life, the *Liturgies* were significant first as a model for two subsequent chamber orchestra works and also because of the stir caused when they were first performed.

Messiaen's style had been nourished by his explorations into ancient, classical, ultramodern, and Hindu techniques, and (according to the composer) by his minute observation of singing birds. He was equally attentive to painting and poetry. Novel harmonic progressions resulting from the invention of modes "of limited transpositions" based on 3, 4, or 5 consecutive notes (alternating half tones and whole tones) selected from the 12-tone chromatic scale and symmetrically extended, uneven rhythm patterns, and many complex devices form the construction of his theory. He also uses a glittering assortment of instruments—celesta, vibraphone, maracas, gong, tam-tam, piano, ondes martenot, and strings—again, in the composer's words—"Europeanized Hindu or Balinese instrumentation."

Parallel to these technical calculations ran an utterly sincere religious sentiment. He dramatized the resplendent imagery of the Catholic religion with elaborate subtitles to his compositions—and viewed each of his works as "an act of faith." He explains himself as desiring "glittering, refined, voluptuous—but not sensuous—music. Music like new blood, a signed gesture, an unknown perfume, an awakened bird!" Music seems to remind him of colors.

One of his works, *Chronochromie*—a word meaning "Color of Time"—has an explanation of color into sound and sound into color that is reminiscent of Scriabin. "When I listen to music," he says, "and even when I read it, I have an inward vision of marvelous colors." *Chronochromie* is colorful. At times it sounds repetitious to a point of attempting jazz. Its real strength and originality—and this should come as no surprise—lies in its orchestral color.

One of Messaien's students, Pierre Boulez (conductor, for a time, of the New York Philharmonic Symphony), has received great praise from his teacher. Boulez disclaims most of modern French music, with the exception of his own and that of his teacher as ''unexportable folklore.'' However, he never lets gratitude interfere with musical opinion, so he eventually turned against Messiaen and condemned his work *Trois Talas* as too ingratiating. Boulez is a revolutionary whose doctrine is dodecaphonic, or atonal (all twelve tones equal, no tonal center) music. Atonal composers, following Schoenberg, saw it as a natural growth and necessary development to emancipate tonality. Critics of the Viennese school call the system disquieting, vaguely alarming, a music for a shattered, belligerent civilization, assaulting the ear like a musical rendition of an aerial bombardment. The atonalists answer that they are freeing music.

In 1913, when Stravinsky's *Sacre du Printemps* had infuriated the Parisian audience, there was a furor because it was felt the work was too modern. In 1945, when his *Four Norwegian Moods* was being performed, there was another furor, only this time it was because the work was too "old-fashioned." The leader of the anti-Stravinsky claque was Pierre Boulez.

Although he was barely twenty, he was already campaigning for dodecaphony. While attending school in Montbrison, he had shown a talent for mathematics. His father, a steel manufacturer, said he should be an engineer. But Boulez was stubborn about a musical career and came to Paris to study at the Paris Conservatoire. The Conservatoire professor who flunked Boulez at his piano examination must have had misgivings when he read reviews about Boulez's pianistic virtuosity. Boulez's technique is so "athletic," he once wore out a Steinway grand in two weeks.

He joined the harmony class of Olivier Messiaen, who is recognized as the most important figure in modern French music before Boulez.

Messiaen had been given a harmony class to teach as a rather perfunctory gesture. Boulez was furious that a man of such musical stature did not have a full professorship in composition. He began to circulate a petition, and when the officials shelved the effort, he left the Conservatoire in disgust, even after winning a first prize in harmony.

As Boulez was separating himself from the Conservatoire, Jean-Louis Barrault was separating himself from the Comédie-Française to found his own theatrical company at the Théâtre Marigny. Barrault hired him despite his brash youthfulness and abrasive opinions. Boulez stayed ten years with the company and orchestrated and conducted music he detested—from Tchaikovsky to Henri Sauguet. Though the relationship was held together with the mortar of mutual respect, Boulez began his celebrated pronouncements: "Schoenberg is dead!" "Any musician who has not felt—and I am not saying understood, but felt—the necessity of the dodecaphonic language is useless."

For Boulez, the cause is clear. Atonal music is not a break with the past but a natural episode in the evolution of musical art, which are the same words used to describe the revolution of Claude Debussy. Boulez' reactions antagonized the French music world and for fifteen years his music was banned from the government-controlled French radio. Every new Boulez work created hostility and controversy. Although the musical establishment was against him, he found private support for the performance of twelve-tone music. In 1954, Barrault allowed Boulez to use a small theater with benches instead of seats to begin a series of concerts to be called the *Domaine Musical.*

The success of these Boulez concerts has implications for today's *relevant* theater. It became fashionable to go and sit on hard wooden benches (using one's mink for a cushion) beside students in blue jeans to listen to the new sounds. Eventually, the *Domaine* moved to larger quarters, and Boulez had given Paris a position of prestige in the music world for the first time since the Ballet Russe had taken refuge there. With the *Domaine* a success, Boulez' role appeared to be changing to one of a counter-establishment leader. Since he loved composing more than conducting, and both more than counterrevolutions, he left Paris.

His most famous compositions are *Le Marteau sans maître* and *Le Soleil des eaux.* His post with the New York Philharmonic began in 1971 and dramatized a curious predicament: Today, the same composer can be booed in his lifetime by one audience because he is too advanced and by another audience becouse he is behind the times. Less than ten years passed between the first performance of Boulez' *Second Piano Sonata,* which was labeled incomprehensible, and *Le Marteau sans maître,* which is condemned by today's young composers as having "soft tone colors and lilting melodies." Such is the way with cultural revolution.

Other figures in the French post-Webern school are Henri Dutilleux, André Jolivet *(Danses Rituelles)* and Maurice Leroux.

For the apostles of *musique concrète* in Paris, Edgard Varèse (1885-1965) became the prophet and patriarch of a whole new dimension in sound. Some critics have felt that as Webern liberated silence, and Schoenberg liberated tonality, Varèse has liberated noise.

Varèse had been a prodigy and a Parisian. At twelve (1897), he composed an opera based on material after Jules Verne. At nineteen (1904), he decided on music as a career, rather than engineering. All his life, however, he continued to study science and technology. (In 1922, he proclaimed that science and music would have to become friends in the future.) His studies under d'Indy, Roussel, and Widor never became a habit with him. He wanted unconditional freedom, and he found it when he went to Berlin where he received musical guidance from Busoni. He was also encouraged by Debussy, Strauss, and Rolland.

He was alert to the discoveries of Stravinsky and Schoenberg, aware of the Futurists, but in 1916 he broke away from their influence; later, in 1955, he disclaimed any debt to them. He began an opera on Hofmannsthal's *Oedipus*. After serving a year in the French army, he came to America (December 1915). He was soon organizing concerts and international societies of new music. Varèse won a certain limited fame with a short list of distinctive works.

In the days before the tape recorder enabled him to work directly on tape, his scores called for instruments that most people thought of as noisemakers: Sirens, chains, anvils, ratchets, clavé sticks, maracas, cowbells, calabashes and *xambomba* (a drum making a sound like a lion's roar). *Ionisation* (1931) is a classic because it produced "electronic" music before the electronic means for it had been invented.

His mature works include *Hyperprism* (1924), for winds and percussion; and *Intégrales* (1926) which constantly shifts metrical units: 5, 4, 2, and 6 and 7 beats to the bar. After a decade, Varèse showed the relevance of his work to the concerns of younger composers by adding: *Déserts,* winds and percussion, with spaced tape recordings of industrial noises and *Poème électronique*.

In *Poème électronique,* Varèse did away with human interpreters and composed directly on tape for Le Corbusier's parabolic Philips pavilion at the 1958 Brussels World's Fair. It was designed to sweep in continuous arcs of sound through approximately four hundred loudspeakers. Its essential connection to Debussy will become apparent with time. Critics do concede it has fascinating elements such as "bleached bones of sound, washed up on the white sands of silence for eight minutes and five seconds."

Varèse cared no more than Debussy for counterpoint. In this respect, especially, he differed from nearly all his contemporaries. On the other hand, he did not subordinate chords and colors to melodic lines. Rather he subordinated both harmonic and melodic intervals to rhythm and sonority. Varèse used unresolved dissonance to produce new shrill sounds. These sounds, when organized in rhythms, suggest energy.

In 1940, Varèse defended his work with this famous explanation: "I prefer to use the expression 'organized sound' and avoid the monotonous question; 'But is it music?' 'Organized sound' seems better to take in the dual aspect of music as an art-science, with all the recent laboratory discoveries which permit us to hope for the unconditional liberation of music, as well as covering, without dispute, my own music in progress and its requirements."

In the 1950s Varèse was hailed as a foremost scout of the *avant-garde,* which now brought him reinforcement. Stravinsky told Craft, "There is nobility in his noise." Odile Vivier claimed a new motivic technique for his work—not development or transformation, but *transmutation.* This seems an excellent word to describe the change of color which electronic machinery made possible and which Varèse knew how to exploit, having heard it within his head, years in advance.

Varèse was only briefly active as a teacher, and his teaching was rather unsystematic. But he was happy to share his ideas with anyone interested and this proved enough to inspire André Jolivet. Study of other composers whose chief work is a valued part of another tradition reveals that many have tried experimenting with new sounds. Varèse made experiment the foundation of all his work and published only his completed achievements.

The label "experimental" was rejected by Varèse, but was accepted by other composers in this field. The term "experimental" seems too convenient to designate a wide variety of music: *musique concrète* (environmental sounds); *musique électronique* (electronically manipulated sounds); and music that involves the computer machine. Somewhere there will emerge Varèse's greatness as a composer. More than any musician of his generation, he was aware of what it meant to be alive in a new time—amid new sounds and new rhythms.

The works of this century cannot be completed without some reference to France's role in the emergence of jazz. Jazz was primarily an American product with a world market. The Afro-American tempo of this idiom found great receptivity in France. In fact, the French musicians and critics were the first to appreciate the seriousness of good jazz. Many composers of this century made use of this style in the streams of their writings.

Hugues Panassié and Robert Goffn showed how to study the history of jazz and André Hodeir showed how to analyze its structure.

The motion picture, the only new art form in the twentieth century, has also contributed to contemporary change. Film, more than any other form of theater except ballet, requires music, and it was inevitable that it would eventually find its own contemporary music, shaped by the musical taste and experience of an enormous contemporary film-going public. George Antheil was one of the composers associated with French music (though he is an American by birth) who sensed the musical potentiality of motion pictures, and he devoted most of his mature career to score writing. In 1936, he had just produced a notable score for *The Plainsman,* and his experiences prompted him to predict that other composers would begin scoring for film, he felt that producers wanted better music because they needed it. The reasons were that it was cheaper to write appropriate musical background than to build an appropriate and authentic background set. The second reason was that the public was becoming accustomed to better-sounding scores.

Antheil's work certainly inspired the sound tracks of *A Man and a Woman* (Francis Lai), and *The Umbrellas of Cherbourg* (Michel LeGrand). Other composers who scored for film were Arthur Honegger, Darius Milhaud, Henri Sauguet, Georges Auric, and Jacques Ibert—all French composers. All were following, unwittingly, in the footsteps of Camille Saint-Saëns, who had composed incidental music for a French film, *L'Assassinat du duc de Guise* (Opus 128), as early as 1908. Another composer who should be added to this list is Lalo Schifrin—now an American, Argentine-born and Paris-trained (Charles Koechlin and Olivier Messiaen). Quincy Jones, whose experience as jazz composer-arranger has been augmented by three years of study with the French teacher of composition, Nadia Boulanger, sees the motion picture as one of the most promising fields for creative expression. Quincy Jones established his reputation in film scoring through his compositions on the following films: *The Pawnbroker, In the Heat of the Night,* and *In Cold Blood.*

The men who dominated the formative years of film scoring were differently trained from the present composers. They were excellent musicians, well versed in traditional techniques of composition and instrumentation, and certainly familiar with the traditional literature, without pretending to be significantly original. The purpose of music in the pictures was to be effective without being obtrusive—and in order to be effective it had also to be familiar. Early sound-track music was reminiscent of Debussy and Ravel—neoclassic composers and dodecaphonic influences were not used. Except for the scoring of "Space" films, electronic music has seldom been used. This may change. For working alongside the symphonically-oriented composers is a still-younger generation of strikingly different background and perspective.

The French popular music scene is very diverse. Artists such as Yves Montand and Serge Reggiani who started out in the 50s still have a considerable audience. They are known for interpreting the poetic and traditional *Chanson française*.

Some *yéyé* singers of the 60s have endured by adapting to various musical fads that came from the United States and England. Johnny Hallyday, Sylvie Vartan and Eddy Mitchell are singers who appear regularly on popular French television variety shows and concerts.

Among the new generation are those groups and singers who are exploring the ground between punk and hard rock and a more subdued French style. Such artists are Alain Souchon, Michel Sardou, and Francis Cabrel. In addition to their own popular musical artists, the French hear a great amount of English-language music on the radio. International artists such as Madonna, Bruce Springsteen, Sting, and Paul McCartney receive significant air-time.

At this point in history, so much has been written about the "new" Renaissance and the cutting edge of change ("There is no avant-garde," says Pierre Boulez, "we are a blotter society!") that future revolutionary trends are as difficult to predict as the present ones are to interpret. However, it might be that France retains her musical resilience because she has survived so many cultural revolutions—or are they constructive adaptations?